NATIONAL SECURITY
AND
DEVELOPMENT
STRATEGY

PERSPECTIVES ON ISLAMIC THOUGHT
Series Editor: Zafar Ishaq Ansari

NATIONAL SECURITY
AND
DEVELOPMENT
STRATEGY

Towards an
Integrated Strategy
for the
Defence and Development
of Pakistan

Arshad Zaman

International Institute of Islamic Thought
Islamabad
1990

First published in Pakistan in 1990
by the International Institute of Islamic Thought, Islamabad

Cataloguing in Publication Data

Zaman, Arshad, 1948--

National Security and Development Strategy.
    (Perspectives on Islamic Thought - 1)

Bibliography : p.
Includes index.

1. Economic Development - Pakistan. 2. Pakistan - Economic Policy. 3. Pakistan - Defence. 4. Economic Development - Religious Aspects - Islam. 5. National security. 6. Social integration. I. Title. II. Series.

ISBN 969-462-000-7   338.95491 dc20

Printed in Pakistan
by
Islamic Research Institute Press
Islamabad

CONTENTS

Foreword i
Preface vii

Introduction xi

1. NATIONAL SECURITY 1

The Meaning of Power 1
The Meaning of Security 2
Assessing Security 3

2. DEVELOPMENT STRATEGY 8

The Meaning of Strategy 8
What is Development Strategy? 9
The Meaning of Development 13

3. THE SEVENTH FIVE-YEAR PLAN [1988-93] 20

Strategy Formulation: Basis and Constraints 21
The Aims of Planning 25
Sixth and Seventh Plans: Growth and Investment 30
Critique, Evaluation and Prospects 32

4. ISLAMICATE TRADITION AND
   POST-COLONIAL SOCIAL STRUCTURE . . 36

The Islamicate Tradition 37
The Colonial Experience and Reaction 50
Post-Colonial Social Structure 53
Implications for National Solidarity 56

5. TOWARD AN INTEGRATED STRATEGY FOR DEFENCE AND DEVELOPMENT .. 58

The Primum Mobile 61
Agreement on Common Ground:
   The Constitution 62
Consensus on Authority:
   On 'Constitutional' Islam 64
Resisting Alien Patronage:
   The Road to Self-Reliance 81
Resisting Coercive Power 85

Annexure: A Brief History of Russian Methods
              of Promoting   Ethno - Linguistic
              Nationalism to Divide the Muslims
              of Soviet Central Asia 94

Notes 103
Bibliography 115

◄►

FOREWORD

The Muslim *ummah* has been engaged, during a good part of this century, in a grim struggle for independence. Doubtlessly that struggle is not quite over. For many Muslim lands, notably Afghanistan, Palestine and Kashmir, continue to languish under foreign dominance; in fact, under downright military occupation. Nevertheless, compared with how things stood in the twenties, the picture of the Muslim world today is, in many respects, much brighter. A vast majority of Muslim lands, some extremely rich in natural resources, are today politically independent. Although things are by no means ideal, there is a revived trend towards unity and co-operation among the Muslim countries. Also, a large section of the *ummah* has been able to overcome the earlier feelings of defeatism and despair regarding the vitality and contemporary relevance of Islam.

The achievement of political liberation by a large number of Muslim countries around the middle of the century stimulated among Muslims the desire to complete the process of their liberation by putting an end to their economic dependence on the developed countries and their exploitation at the hands of the latter. No less important, however, was the desire to achieve cultural liberation, the desire to live according to one's vision of life; the desire to live naturally, to live a life that is one's own. This process reached a high mark during the seventies and eighties when the world witnessed what has been described as "Islamic resurgence". This consists essentially of the popular desire of the Muslims to see Islamic ideals translated into practice so that they are reflected in individual conduct, collective behaviour, and state policies. Notwithstanding the misunderstanding to which this phenomenon gave rise among non-Muslims, it was a natural concomitant of political independence. For freedom and independence are meaningless if they do not enable a people to affirm and assert their identity. Be that as it may, in recent years there has been a vigorous search for roots throughout the Muslim world, a strong insistence on developing laws and institutions consistent with the spirit and characteristics of the Muslim society.

At this stage of Muslim history, a heavy responsibility devolves on Muslim scholars and thinkers. Ever since the *ummah*'s encounter with Western civilization, Muslim scholars have been devoting their energy mainly to the achievement of a few vital goals.

Through their writings they have attempted to establish the excellence and merit of Islam as a religious system and as a way of life. They have also defended Islam against the criticism mounted by both anti-Islamic religious missionaries and westernized secularists. In short, Muslim scholarly effort has been directed, in the main, to restoring and reinforcing the faith of Muslims in Islam as a sound and viable system of life.

The task to which Muslim scholars and thinkers should seriously address themselves now is of a more vital and creative character than the one to which their attention has so far been devoted. For it consists of presenting an alternative to the dominant materialist civilization of the age. Muslim rulers and politicians are often blamed for their failure to effectively advance the cause of Islam. The fact of the matter, however, is that the failure of the Muslim scholars and thinkers is as much if not more consequential. For at the present stage of world history when the throne of the entire secular philosophy of life seems to be tottering, it is tragic that sustained attempts have scarcely been made by Muslim scholars to present the Islamic alternative to traditional religious beliefs and practices as well as to Western secular civilization which has come to prevail over the whole world.

The International Institute of Islamic Thought has been trying to mobilize Islamic scholarship to the creative task mentioned above. The present monograph, which is a slightly revised version of a paper presented by Dr. Arshad Zaman in a seminar held under the auspices of the Institute in Islamabad early this year, is an effort in that direction.

Dr. Zaman is a well-known economist of Pakistan. A major characteristic of the Islamic vision, which both inspires and underlies Dr. Zaman's work, is its pervasive view of life. According to this view life, with its different aspects, is seen essentially as a unity. The different aspects of life may be considered separately for analytical purposes provided the over-all unity of life is not allowed to be obscured.

This pervasive approach is reflected in Dr. Zaman's attempt to develop an integrated strategy for the national security and economic development of Pakistan. The underlying assumption of Dr. Zaman's approach is the recognition of vital interconnections not only between national security and economic development but also between these and the nation's world-view and vision of life, its commonly accepted norms of behaviour, and the realities of its historic experience reflected in its social, economic and cultural life. It is a measure of this approach that Dr. Zaman has also highlighted the sharp polarization between the 'vernacular' and 'anglophile' classes in the post-colonial period as an integral part of his concern for security and development. Also, while recommending the measures that ought to be adopted the author has compellingly shown that the objectives of national security and economic development cannot be achieved by concentrating attention and effort exclusively on those objectives. Concern for those objectives, in this view, also calls for taking active interest in a variety of fields which short-sighted specialists usually tend to ignore on the plea that they are irrelevant. Dr. Zaman considers the achievement of those objectives to be contingent on such seemingly unrelated questions as the development of a consensus on authority, the design and implementation of a national policy on culture, the recognition of the central importance of the *shari* vision, and so on.

The present monograph, in fact the entire effort of the International Institute of Islamic Thought, is aimed at generating fresh thinking among Muslims from an Islamic frame of reference. There are no pretensions to monopoly of wisdom, no claims to intellectual finality, let alone infallibility. The underlying spirit of our activity is the conviction that every sincere and responsible intellectual effort will be of service to the cause of Islam in so far as it is likely to stimulate further effort among scholars. Thus, we hope that gradually there will be more light and greater clarity in regard to Islamic imperatives for human thought and action in this changed world of ours.

It is in this spirit that this first of a series of monographs on Islamic thought is being presented. And it is being done with fervent prayer to Allah that He may dispel darkness and direct us all to the light of His Guidance.

Zafar Ishaq Ansari

Islamabad
Rabī' al-Thānī 1410
November 1989

PREFACE

This unintended monograph has developed from very modest beginnings. In September 1988, I was invited to speak on Development Strategy for Pakistan at the National Defence College course on The Economy as an Element of National Power. In preparing my talk, delivered on September 26, 1988, I tried to address the problem of how development strategy could enhance national security.

In doing so, I made extensive notes from several standard elementary books on a variety of subjects, mainly to clarify my own thoughts. The intent was not scholarly exposition, but the elaboration of a practical course of action, on the basis hopefully of cogent arguments. This fundamental objective remains in the present monograph.

The lecture had a mixed reception. One or two students, however, made persistent requests for a write-up. In response, in October and November 1988, I wrote up the talk, relying extensively on my notes to buttress the position I had taken. In addition to the students, the paper was circulated to a number of friends and was presented at a seminar organized by the International Institute of Islamic Thought in Islamabad on January 25, 1989.

This monograph is essentially an updated version of the paper presented at the seminar. Although the temptation to revise the paper quite substantially in the light of subsequent events and some changes in my own views has been great, I have resisted it.

The monograph relies primarily on published materials to set out definitions of concepts and categories, historical accounts and constructs, and analyses of various issues which have been adapted to our context, to provide a basis for recommendations contained in the last chapter.

As due credit may not have been given in the main text, it may be best to acknowledge the main sources on which much of the exposition draws (often, extensively): J. K. Galbraith (on power), E. N. Luttwak and A. O. Hirschman (on strategy), Barrington Moore, Jr. and Simon Kuznets (on the history and economics of modernization and development), Marshall G. S. Hodgson (on Islamic history and institutions), S. M. Ikram (on the history of Pakistan), Alexandre Bennigsen and his colleagues (on Soviet Central Asia) and Henry Kissinger (on the need for a security doctrine). Much of this should have appeared properly within quotation marks. In order not to impair the readability of the text, however, this has not been done. Instead, sources have been indicated in notes to the text at the end of the monograph.

I should also acknowledge my debt to works in Urdu, which have not been cited. In many ways, these works have contributed to the structure of my (admittedly limited) understanding of the Muslim heritage of Pakistan, which is reflected indirectly in the monograph. In particular, I would like to mention Maulana Abul Ḥasan 'Alī Nadawī's *Tārīkh-i-Da'wat wa 'Azimat* (and his other works) and S. M. Ikram's famous *Kawthar* trilogy.

A number of friends and colleagues not only read earlier versions of the paper and commented on it, but encouraged me to publish it. Among them, helpful comments from Tariq Banuri, Ijaz S. Gilani, Noor A. Husain, A. R. Kemal, Waqar M. Khan, M. Tariq Siddiqi and Khalid N. Soofi are gratefully acknowledged. Maulana Yusuf Talal Ali was kind enough to go over the section on Islam, to see that no serious error of interpretation had been made. I should also record my gratitude to Zafar Ishaq Ansari, without whose persuasion and persistent efforts, the monograph would never have been published. They are all, of course, neither necessarily in agreement with the views expressed here, nor responsible for any of the remaining errors.

I am also indebted to Kamal Matinuddin, who was kind enough to return the paper with extensive editorial corrections, most of which I have incorporated. Finally, I am grateful to Sohail Rehan and Muhammad Saeed for their painstaking efforts in preparing the manuscript for publication.

Arshad Zaman

Islamabad
May 31, 1989

INTRODUCTION

It is among the paradoxes of our times that in an atmosphere rife with war, threats of war, international distrust, extortion, subversion, insurgencies, terrorism, and defences against them, every discussion of economic development proceeds on the assumption of peace, prosperity and economic cooperation.[1] It is the purpose of this monograph to discuss development strategy, primarily as it relates to Pakistan, under more realistic assumptions about the potential for conflict. In particular, it addresses the question of how development strategy can be used to enhance national security.

In order to lend some precision to the discussion, national security, and development strategy, together with the associated concepts of power and strategy, are defined in chapters 1 and 2. With the aid of these concepts, the development strategy pursued in Pakistan (including that in the Seventh Five-Year Plan) is examined in chapter 3. We find that there has not been any strategy (in any meaningful sense of the term) which has been pursued. In part, this is because the abilities and inclinations of our planners have been determined more by foreign influences than by any familiarity with or confidence in their own society. chapters 4 and 5 attempt to provide a brief description of our own heritage and an outline of an approach to a security-enhancing strategy of economic development.

Chapter 1

NATIONAL SECURITY

National security is a complex concept in which military strength and national power are but constitutive elements, even though important ones. To begin with, therefore, it is important to arrive at a concrete understanding of the meaning of power, security, and national security.

The Meaning of Power[1]

Power is the ability to influence the behaviour of others, in accordance with one's will, whether those influenced act voluntarily or involuntarily. In this, three aspects of power can be distinguished:

(i)   authority, which brings about a voluntary (or conditioned) submission by others;

(ii)   patronage, which induces others to obey in the hope of material advantage; and

(iii)   coercive ability, which induces others by their desire to avoid pain.[2]

The successful use of power depends on the total psychological make-up of both the subject and the object of power, and the interaction of this make-up in situations of conflict. Corresponding to the three attributes of the subject of power, the object of power may be motivated by love (or respect, or loyalty); or greed (or avarice); or fear.

Obedience to authority is, and can be, conditioned by upbringing, education, and propaganda. Unlike patronage and coercion, which are highly visible means of persuasion, authority is subjective and hidden, evoked by images and symbols, and lies in the realm of morality and psychology, dealing with charisma, personality, and style.[3] Patronage, related to property and wealth, is in the realm of the economic, dealing with grants of land, or land revenue, or licenses, permits, and quotas, or exemptions from payment of taxes and duties. Finally, coercive ability, dealing with detention, confinement, and brutality, is related to organization, the most important source of power in modern (meaning European[4]) societies.

The Meaning of Security

In a hostile environment, security arises from the capability to oppose power. In most cases, the opposition is symmetric, where the response to the instruments of power (authority, patronage and coercion) and its sources (symbols, property and organization) is a build-up of these same attributes. But it can also be asymmetric, where for example an overwhelmingly organized coercive power is opposed by resort to authority and personality—a glorious example being Quaid-e-Azam Mohammad Ali Jinnah's struggle against the British colonialists and the Indian nationalists.[5] The permutations and combinations of asymmetric response can be many. The success of asymmetric response is the subject of strategy—which when successful, can be the stuff of legend.

In addition to a direct opposition of power, whether symmetric or asymmetric, hostile power can be opposed by indirect means as well. This is the realm of diplomacy, which seeks first, to reduce the strength of the instruments of hostile power by isolating the enemy from international support, and second, to enhance defensive power, by bringing into play international support of the instruments of defensive power.

As the strategic environment for the Third World conflict has increasingly come to be of the nature of what has been called coalition warfare, the role of diplomacy has become paramount.[6] As it would take us too far afield, however, we shall not say more about diplomacy.

Assessing Security

In assessing security, therefore, it is essential to arrive at an assessment of the source, type, and mix, of power which is to be opposed, and its likely use. Unfortunately, the military establishment which deals with threat assessment tends to think overwhelmingly in terms of the threat of an all-out invasion. It prepares for it mainly by assessing relative strengths and readiness states, setting force goals and troops/terrain ratios, acquiring weapons systems, providing tactical training and preparing operational plans. While the importance of these activities should not be underrated, the task of meeting more limited but far more effective threats to national security [in terms of propaganda, subversion, encouragement of insurgencies, etc.] slips between the conventional division of responsibilities in modern bureaucratic states.

Based on a study of recent wars between smaller powers, it has been concluded that in future wars four major patterns can be expected (Cohen 1987, pp. 16-19):

(i)   *Predominance of the surprise, set-piece, but limited offensive*, with the intent of bringing about a favourable settlement, as opposed to conventional warfare aimed at decisive victory: the examples given, being the Chinese intervention in Vietnam, the Argentine seizure of the Falkland/Malvinas, the Israeli invasion of Lebanon, and earlier, the Indian invasion of East Pakistan in 1971.

(ii)   *Attrition warfare*, which may be intentional or unintentional, and is a direct consequence of the first operational characteristic—the sudden but limited offensive, especially where the attacker miscalculates, as was the case in the Iran-Iraq war.

(iii)   *Resort to unconventional means of warfare*
          as a supplement to conventional ground
          offensive: for example, the use of chemical
          weapons in the Iran-Iraq war; and the
          encouragement of insurgencies, such as the
          Indian use of the Mukti Bahini in 1971, and
          terrorist activities.

(iv)   *Urbanization of warfare* in which major
          battles ta'ke place in large and important
          cities, as demonstrated in Khorramshahr,
          Beirut, and Lang Son–and as would seem to
          have been the Indian intent in their abortive
          push towards Lahore in 1965.[7]

Keeping these factors in mind, we may examine the
factors affecting Pakistan's security position, as follows:

(i)   *Security from Coercion*: In terms of troops to
          terrain ratios and relative strength, our
          primary source of threat, India, enjoys an
          overwhelming superiority over Pakistan,
          which we simply do not have the resources
          to match to any degree. This is especially
          true in the light of the major build-up of
          defence that has taken place in India in the
          last few years. In this area, our strategy must
          continue to be to rely on good intelligence
          to guard against a surprise pre-emptive
          attack (on the ground, in the air and on the

high seas), modern combat materiel and superior tactical abilities of our forces, which have served us well in previous engagements.[8]

(ii)   *Security from Economic Influence*:   Our primary vulnerability to economic influence arises from the need for modern weapons, which forces us into dependent relations with the United States, primarily, and with other North Atlantic Treaty Organization (NATO) countries secondarily. The United States has made it clear to us on more than one occasion that its defence relations with us are to help resist Soviet, not Indian, moves against us; it has also exerted pressure on us to adopt a policy of appeasement towards India.

(iii)   *Security from Submission to Alien Authority*: By far the most effective use of power is the cultivation of the belief that the act of submission is not under duress, but is voluntary and self-initiated. It is here that we have not even begun to appreciate the threat: in the battle for minds there is no Pakistani presence to speak of--whatever we think is either US-British inspired, or Soviet-Indian inspired. For different reasons, both are united in their opposition to Islam, and in their support of a policy of promoting divisive ethno-linguistic tendencies; as a result, aided by our own neglect of equitable domestic policies, today the lack of national unity has become the greatest threat to our security.

We shall have occasion to examine development strategy in terms of these specific threats to our security. To begin to do so, however, requires a more precise understanding of the meaning of development strategy, the subject of the next chapter.

Chapter 2

DEVELOPMENT STRATEGY

Having arrived at a concrete understanding of power and national security, we can turn to a similar effort to define what we mean by strategy, development strategy, and indeed, economic development, before examining the question of an economic development strategy for Pakistan, and its relation to national security.

The Meaning of Strategy[1]

The idioms and metaphors of war have had a Powerful hold on human imagination. Strategy is one of those words which originates in military use, but has found ready use in numerous contexts in which human action takes place in complex circumstances.

On its home ground, however, strategy refers to a situation not only of complexity, but one in which commonsense (minimum-effort) action suggested by ordinary logic becomes inappropriate; instead action based on a paradoxical and contradictory logic is thought to lead to a desired result. Perhaps the most obvious example of this is provided in the logic of deterrence: to defend, you must be ready to attack; to be ready to attack is evidence of peaceful intent; to prepare defences, is aggressive, or at least provocative (Luttwak 1987,p. 4).

Two elements are central to strategy, in the military sense. First, the presence of an opposing will, the enemy, who is not only aware of you and your intentions, but anticipates your moves, and seeks to reverse them by a variety of means. Second, the success, as a result, of paradoxical and contradictory actions, where actions motivated by ordinary linear logic would have failed.[2]

What is Development Strategy?

The term 'development strategy' is seldom used in this full-bodied sense. The word strategy was introduced into discussion of economic development and development planning in the context of what in retrospect proved to be a not very productive debate which was current in the late 1950s. The prevailing view then was that economic growth, despite its limitations, was in fact synonymous with economic development (at least for all practical purposes), and growth depended on investment. In this context, the conventional wisdom was that investment resources should be allocated across all sectors so as to promote 'balanced growth' of all sectors together.[3]

The concern was that uncoordinated investment could be self-defeating. It was felt that industry should not get too far ahead of agriculture. Infrastructure [called 'social overhead capital' in those days] must keep pace with industry. Finally, in the then famous 'shoe factory' example given earlier by Rosenstein-Rodan [1943], it was argued that by itself, setting up a shoe factory in an underdeveloped country would be of no use because the workers, employees and owners of the factory would not buy all its products, and the rest of the economy would be too poor to afford shoes! So, unless everything was done together, nothing could be done at all.

In this milieu, in an influential book entitled *The Strategy of Economic Development*, an American economist, Albert Hirschman argued that paradoxical as it may sound, there may be some virtue in purposely creating imbalances in order to foster growth.[4] The argument was that where 'pressures, tensions, and disequilibriums' create difficulties, they are at the same time the stimulus for responses which create development.

The growth of any industry induces investment in input-supplying industries [through 'backward linkages'] and, where the industry does not satisfy final demand, in output-using industries [through 'forward linkages']. These linkages vary in strength. Therefore, by concentrating investment in sectors with strong linkages, an unbalanced growth may give rise, in time, to rapid balanced growth, which may not come about if balanced growth was pursued to begin with.

The actual details of the controversy are not so important today. In the context of the present discussion, however, it should be noted that in Hirschman's scheme of things, there was no active enemy seeking to foil the planner's objective. Development strategy was strategy only in the sense of involving a paradoxical logic which was associated with strategy in its original sense.

Since Hirschman, however, it became fashionable to speak of development strategy–in the sense of advocating a certain pattern of sectoral growth, and by implication, investment; although gradually, even the sense of paradox has been lost. Today, in most cases when we speak of development strategy, we don't speak of strategy at all. In most cases what is meant is merely a consistent, well-thought plan of action.

There are, however, contexts in which development strategy is used in a sense which is much closer to its origins. The use of development strategy, in the original sense, as a paradoxical stratagem against opposing forces, occurs in the literature on central planning.

In China, for example, Mao Zedong [1965, p. 165] put forward the following strategy of land reform which began in 1950:

First, the demands of the poor peasants and farm laborers must be satisfied; this is the most fundamental task in the land reform. Second, there must be firm unity with the middle peasants, and their interests must not be damaged. As long as we grasp these two principles, we can certainly carry out our tasks in the land reform successfully.

Here, the strategy was to launch an attack on the landlords, by using the poor peasants and farm labourers, while neutralizing the rich peasantry, whose premature opposition could ruin the strategy. The tactical principles underlying this strategy, identifying clearly whom to rely on, whom to unite, whom to neutralize and whom to attack, consisted of:[6]

- *Placing reliance, in the rural areas, on the poor peasants and farm labourers*, who were already irreconciliably antagonistic towards the large landholder [and the feudal system]; who needed land more urgently than any other class; and who, being most oppressed, were the most militant.

  Uniting the well-to-do middle peasants, who were both labourers and small private owners, about whom Mao Zedong had said that 'The positive or negative attitude of the middle peasants is one of the factors determining victory or defeat in the revolution' and for whom the 1950 Land Reform Law stipulated that: 'the land and property of the middle peasants, should be protected against violation.'

- *Neutralizing the rich peasants*, who unlike the landlords, were felt first, to practice a 'less severe' form of exploitation, and second, to work their lands themselves to some degree; thus, reducing 'the scale of the target of attack' in rural areas and lessening the resistance to land reform.
- *Liquidating the landlord class*, while allowing individual landlords who offered no resistance to retain 'the same amount of land as available to peasants' but compelling them 'to reform themselves through physical labour.'

Development strategy, then, has been used in two senses. It has meant the identification of linkages in an effort to determine a pattern of investment which would maximize growth. Alternatively, it has also meant the planning of social change, taking into account the likely reaction of the social classes involved.

The Meaning of Development

No matter how we think of development strategy, we must also be clear in our minds about the aim of development strategy. What does it mean for the strategy to succeed? In other words, what is development? There are two approaches to answering this question. One, historical, based mainly on developments in Europe (and also in Japan) over the course of some 150 years prior to World War I. The other, logical (favoured by most modern economists), based on an extract of the essence of this experience.

History: Three Routes to Development   In terms of European history, a distinction can be made between three alternative routes that were taken to the so-called 'modern' world, depending on the social class which spearheaded the movement to modernize:[6]

(i)   *Bourgeois Revolution [Democracy]*, which took place in England, France and the United States of America, in which first, secular values triumphed over religion, and second, a bloody revolution took place in all three countries in which fundamental conflicts over values and over questions of social and political philosophy were settled. On the basis of this democratic revolution, three things were accomplished: arbitrary rulers were checked; arbitrary rules were replaced by just, rational and objective laws, through the establishment of the rule of law and the power of the legislature; and finally, mechanisms were established by which the people could influence the making of these rules, such as the right to vote, freedom of speech, the right to peaceful assembly, and lastly, the use of the state to provide for the welfare of the people.

(ii) *Revolution from Above [Fascism],* which was next in historical sequence, took place mainly in Germany, but also in Italy and Spain [and in Japan in Asia]. These countries were able to avoid the bloody revolution which was characteristic of the other two paths, by the use of traditional social relationships and attitudes to bring about a peaceful revolution from above, in which big industry and big agriculture were promoted at the expense of agricultural labour, peasants and consumers. On this basis, four things were accomplished: a strong central government, a powerful bureaucracy, and a uniform administrative system were created; a uniform law code and system of courts was established; a military machine powerful enough to matter internationally was built up on a scale large enough to stimulate heavily tariff-protected industrialization; and agriculture and industry were transformed into capitalist forms, by preserving customary social arrangements to keep peasant and labour wages low.

(iii) *Peasant Revolution [Communism],* historically, the last route to the modern world, was the path taken by Russia and China in the twentieth century, leading to the establishment of communism. Although the conditions and accomplishments of the two countries were quite distinct, in both Russia and China, the establishment of the communist order was preceded by a bloody revolution with origins mainly but not exclusively in the peasantry.

Logic: The Patterns of Development   From an ahistorical, logical point of view, the following features were distilled from the European experience (excluding the communist countries), as being characteristic of development [a process, which after World War II, was held up to Afro-Asian and Latin American countries, for them to emulate]:[7]

(i)   *The development of a secular, egalitarian, nationalist outlook*: meaning, by secular, a 'concentration on life on earth,...as contrasted with a view of life on earth as a brief transitional phase which deserves relatively little attention'; by egalitarian, a view of all human beings being inherently equal, except in their activity potential; and by nationalism, a 'community of feeling, grounded in a common historical past and its cultural heritage.'

(ii)   *A sustained* [over a minimum of thirty to forty years] *and marked increase not only in per capita product but also in population.*[8]

(iii)   *A change in industrial structure*, by which is meant a change in the shares in production and employment of the various sectors: first, a move away from agriculture [called industrialization], in which the share of agriculture in total output falls from any-where between 50-66% to under 20%; second, a change within industry proper [mining, manufacturing and construction], with a rise in the share of manufacturing [including or excluding power, gas, and water], from 20-30% to 40-50%; and, finally, shifts in the structure of the services sector.

(iv)   *Changes in the distribution of product and income*: first, as a share of national income, a decline in personal income of households [compensated, however, by transfer payments by government and business], and a rise in depreciation, net indirect taxes, and pre-tax post-dividend corporate income accruing to non-personal organizations [government and corporations]; second, an eventual decline [after a period of stability] in property income of households [dividends, interest and rent–including imputed rent on owner-occupied housing], and especially in returns to owners' equity; third, a rise in the share of labour, as a counterpart both to the decline in the share of capital, and to gains attributable to greater investment in the training and education of labour; and fourth, a decline in income inequality (in the size distribution of income) after an initial period of stability, or even a rise.

(v)   *Changes in the patterns of product use, in which*: first, as a share of gross national income, government consumption, which includes defence and administration, rises (from about 3.5-5% to about 14%), capital formation [or investment] stays the same or rises (from under 10% to some 12-20%, or more), and private consumption declines (from over 80% to about 60%); second, the share of personal savings probably rises (the historical trends are mixed) from about 2-5% to almost 10% of disposable income— with households, even including individual proprietors, contributing only about a half of national savings, so that the public sector and the private corporate sector, together, contribute at least as much as households

and entrepreneurs; and third, consumer
expenditures per capita keep pace with the
rise in disposable income per capita, while
unexpectedly, both the share of expenditure
on food does not fall, and that on clothing,
does not rise—but the trends are mixed,
probably because of three factors: changes
in living conditions (including most con-
spicuously, the complex changes associated
with rapid urbanization), technological
changes (inducing higher consumption levels,
of canned and frozen food, synthetic fibre
textiles, electrical appliances and other
consumer durables, automobiles, air transportation, and newer products like telephones),
and changes in occupational composition of
the active population which affects income
distribution and the pattern of consumption.
With this understanding of the meaning of development and the two senses in which development strategy
has been used we can turn to an examination of development strategy in Pakistan, and see how development
strategy has been related to national security.

Chapter 3

THE SEVENTH FIVE-YEAR PLAN
[1988-93]

Three points can be made about planning in general, and economic planning in particular, in Pakistan:

(i) First, planning for development and for security takes place without any reference to each other—in fact, even security is not addressed in an integrated way: diplomacy and defence, though linked, proceed quite separately, and defence itself, is only loosely coordinated between the primary tasks assigned to each service.[1]

(ii) Second, with the possible exception of the Third Five-Year Plan (when an effort was made to exploit linkages), it is safe to say that there has never been any development strategy, in the full sense of the term, underlying any of our five-year plans.[2]

(iii) Third, that the Seventh Plan is no exception.

Strategy Formulation: Basis and Constraints

The basis for national planning in Pakistan is the Constitution. Within this framework, however, the constraints to the formulation of a development strategy, in any meaningful sense of the term, arise from three sources: the overriding importance of the budgetary process; the rivalry between ministries engaged in plan formulation; and, even more importantly, between the federation and the provinces.

The Constitutional Basis Pakistan has a federal constitution in which, together with defence and diplomacy, development planning is a federal subject—that is, the power to make laws in this area resides with the federation. In the area of planning the federal list contains the following description of the subject:

> National planning and national economic coordination including planning and coordination of scientific and technological research. [Article 70(4), Fourth Schedule, Part I, item 32.]

The Constitution [Article 156] also provides for the President to constitute a National Economic Council, chaired by the Prime Minister, and members to be nominated by the President, including one member each to be nominated by the provinces.[3] Under the Constitution:

> The National Economic Council shall review the overall economic condition of the country and

shall, for advising the Federal Government and the Provincial Governments, formulate plans in respect of financial, commercial, social and economic policies; and in formulating such plans, it shall be guided by the Principles of Policy set out in Chapter 2 of Part II.[4]

The Constitution takes an unusually ambivalent position on what are called the Principles of Policy [Articles 29-40]: whereas all organs of the State [including persons acting on its behalf] are directed to act in accordance with these Principles [Art. 29(1)], it is explicitly provided that these Principles are to be followed only if resources are available [Art. 29(2)], and that no action or law can be called into question merely because it departs from these Principles [Art. 30(2)]. Thus, Principles are to be followed subject to availability of resources, and no remedies are to lie against the state if they are not followed!

It is the National Economic Council therefore which is charged by the Constitution to formulate plans on behalf of the federation, and in doing so, is to be guided by these Principles of Policy. While the National Economic Council approves the plan, the Planning Commission [in theory[5]] and the economic and technical staff of the Planning and Development Division [in practice] prepare the plan document. The Minister for Planning and Development and the Deputy Chairman,

Planning Commission often play a significant role in the conceptual design of the plans.

The Primacy of the Budget   The single most important issue in the formulation of all plans is the availability of resources, which determines the overall size of the plan. The bulk of the effort of the Ministry of Planning is exerted to secure the agreement of the Ministry of Finance to as high a budgetary appropriation for the Plan as possible. The intensity of this struggle between the planning and finance ministries, with sophisticated tactical manoeuvres by the finance ministry to delay agreement on the resource position until the very last minute, precludes any attention being given to strategy formulation.

The scope for major changes in the development programme is never there to begin with, but the budgetary process ensures that a serious effort to rethink strategy by fundamentally revising development schemes, or altering inter-sectoral priorities, is not made. Each ongoing project is a line item of the budget which is a potential bid for resources. Any effort to redraw the plan by discarding bad projects and inserting new ones, risks certain loss of resources allocated to development, without any guarantee of additionality.

Inter-Ministerial Rivalry   A second impediment to strategy formulation is the rivalry between finance and planning ministries on the one hand, and executing ministries on the other, for authority to determine priorities and for maximal share of resources. For example, the Ministry of Water and Power correctly sees its prime task to be the stable supply of energy to all consumers. It rightly argues for free access to imported raw materials and intermediate goods. The Ministry of Industries, a user of energy, will insist on unlimited supplies of energy, but would argue that WAPDA should not be allowed to import those goods which domestic industry can supply. A resolution of these conflicts at the strategic level seldom takes place.

Centre-Province Rivalry   Finally, as the relative strength of the federation versus the provinces varies, there is a tug of war for control over plan formulation and execution between the centre, charged by the Constitution for national planning, and the provinces, charged by the Constitution for the bulk of plan execution. Over the years, federal programmes in areas clearly allocated to the provinces [especially education, but also health, and other social sectors] have grown rapidly, to the point that high priority provincial schemes are either not funded or remain under-funded.

Additional difficulties in centre-province relations are created by political delays in the implementation of the Constitution's provisions for sharing of revenues, water, and exhaustible natural resources (or royalties from them). Naturally, these are not without implications for the process of plan formulation itself.

The Aims of Planning

With this perspective, two observations can be made about national planning in Pakistan: first, that the Ministry of Planning constitutes a very narrow base for the expression of national concerns; and second, that the nature of planning, to borrow military terminology, becomes more tactical than strategic. In order of importance, then, the chief aims of planning are: mobilizing foreign loans and grants; providing an input into domestic politics (by providing a basis for securing support for the government from both public representatives and the electorate); and last, and least important, as a genuine plan for allocation of resources for the achievement of development objectives.

Mobilizing Foreign Assistance   The link between planning and foreign 'assistance' has always been a close and strong one. In Pakistan, the close association of the Planning Commission with the Ford Foundation, and subsequently the Harvard Advisory Group [1953-70] and the United States International Cooperation Agency [now, the U. S. Agency for International Development] is well-known.[6]   Over the years, these links have weakened, and have shifted from bilateral to multilateral agencies [mainly, the International Monetary Fund, the World Bank, and the Asian Development Bank], but the patterns and procedures of planning remain much the same.

Also, international lenders, as well as bilateral sources of development finance, often require that formal economic plans be prepared, to support a programme of foreign loans and grants. It is not surprising therefore that the primary, overriding, aim of all plans in Pakistan (as elsewhere) has been as a document to support a request for foreign assistance. In this, our plans have been highly successful. The last, Sixth Five-Year Plan, was able to mobilize US$ 5.1 billion of assistance from Consortium countries, which was over two-thirds above the US$ 3.1 billion, mobilized for the Fifth Plan. Similarly, the Seventh Plan envisages the mobilization of US$ 8.1 billion in foreign assistance.

An important consequence of this situation is that in these circumstances a development plan cannot be a plan for self-reliance, for the simple reason that the plan as an aid request must demonstrate a large gap in intended spending and domestic resources. Any plan for self-reliance, on the other hand, would be a poor case for seeking foreign assistance, as it would show a very small foreign assistance requirement (if any). This is simply a reflection of the fact that since World War II international financial assistance has been available not by way of disinterested help, but primarily as an instrument of the foreign policy of governments providing this assistance.

Planning as an Input to Politics In addition to being an output of international politics, a clear, secondary role of planning and plan preparation, shared as an objective by both the foreign 'donors' and domestic governments, has been the use of development spending to support domestic politics. Once again, the history of this process is closely associated since the early 1950s with various rural development programmes, the rural works schemes, and the development of local government institutions, all with active participation of U.S. experts.

More recently, during the Sixth Plan period, Prime Minister Junejo's Five-Point Programme was an especially high-profile effort to link the Sixth Plan to the political government's programme.[7] Similarly, in response to the rising criticism of government for failing to provide [essentially, government] employment to matriculates and graduates, the Seventh Plan provides a small lump-sum allocation to be used for employment programmes, to be conceived in due course. As an input to politics, then, plans provide for extending patronage to political representatives [in return, presumably, for political support], to win voter support in the constituencies, and to defuse criticism of economic policies.

Planning for Development Burdened with these two superior objectives, there is little scope left for the plan to be an effective instrument of husbanding scarce resources to projects in accordance with national priorities. In any event, the plan itself is of little practical import. Procedurally, the allocation of funds to development schemes takes place in the context of annual development programmes, as part of the budget. Substantively, with budgetary resources always scarce, aid availability is usually the deciding criterion of project selection. Policies are made in the context of specific cases, which are decided on quite separate considerations. The plan therefore serves mainly as a reference document to provide a general framework for economic decision-making, which is observed more in the breach than in observance.

The failure of plans, as exercises in serious planning, can be illustrated by comparing planned allocations to actual development expenditures. In the Sixth Plan for example, sectors showing the widest variations

between planned and actual allocation of funds (as %
shares of total investment) were as follows:

Table 1

Planned vs. Actual Sectoral Priorities

	Planned	Actual
Agriculture & Fertilizer Subsidy	4.7	7.1
Mining & Industry	8.6	6.2
Energy	27.2	21.8
(of which: Power)	(9.3)	(9.9)
Physical Planning & Housing	4.7	10.0
Rural Roads	0.6	1.6
Special Development Programme	5.2	1.5

Source: Planning and Development Division.

Sixth and Seventh Plans: Growth and Investment

With these limitations in mind, it nevertheless may be useful, for the record, to review the sectoral composition of the investment and growth targets of the Sixth and Seventh Five-Year Plans (Table 2).

Table 2

Planned and Actual Growth, by Sectors

	Fifth Plan		Sixth Plan		7th Plan
	Target	Actual	Target	Actual	Target
Agriculture	6.0	4.4	4.9	3.8	4.7
Manufacturing	10.0	9.0	9.3	7.7	8.1
Construction	8.4	7.1	8.5	8.7	8.0
Electricity & Gas	*	9.0	8.0	8.8	8.5
Transport & Communication	*	7.0	6.8	8.2	7.7
Other Sectors	6.6	7.0	6.1	7.2	6.4
GDP (fc)	7.0	6.6	6.5	6.5	6.5
Memo:					
Public Sector as % of Total Investment	70.5	65.5	59.2	59.5	58.9

* not available

Source:Planning and Development Division.

It should be clear from these figures that industry has been viewed as the leading sector, which would spearhead economic growth (whether defined in its proper sense—as mining, manufacturing and construction, or in its extended sense—including also, power and transport). Secondly, there has been a degree of optimism in the setting of the agricultural growth target, although it has been tempered by the experience of decelerating growth rates. Finally, in response to the major effort to shift the burden of investment and growth to the private sector during the Sixth Plan, public sector development outlays have decreased as a share of total investment [from about 66% to 60%]. At the same time, the rate of economic growth (both target and achieved) has been high.

The setting of growth targets, of course, is of lesser practical consequence than the setting of investment targets. In particular, it is the public sector investment allocation which is of direct consequence to resource allocation. Private sector investment targets are expected to be achieved indirectly, by the design of a policy framework designed to bring about the desired allocation. The sectoral shares of investment, indicative of inter-sectoral priorities, are shown in Table 3 below.

Some interesting conclusions can be derived from a comparison of the two tables. First, even though the leading sector of planned growth is industry, its share in planned investment is both low and declining. Obviously, the bulk of industrial growth is expected to take place in the private sector (and is taking place, more because of government policies than because of direct public investment). Second, despite a somewhat lower and constant planned share, the share of private investment in physical planning and housing (mainly residential construction) has declined (from roughly one-fourth to one-fifth). But public construction during the Sixth Plan has been substantially in excess of both past trends and plan targets (probably, largely due to housing under Prime Minister Junejo's Five-Point Programme).

Critique, Evaluation and Prospects

The fundamental criticism of the Sixth and Seventh Plans, as of earlier plans, is the absence of any meaningful development strategy. Instead they have reflected the fashions in thinking on development as they have evolved in countries that have provided us with development finance.[8] This must not, however, blind us to the fact that the undeniable success of plans to mobilize foreign assistance, in a period when weak political institutions have precluded the ability of governments to raise taxes, has been essential to maintain political stability and promote economic well-being. The question is, whether there is a better way?

This question, too, is not new. It has been asked before, almost since the beginning of the debate on development, and the answer that we must find 'our own way' has been repeated ritually.[9] The problem has been twofold: first, the intellectual and social background of our planners and decision-makers has been heavily influenced by Western modes of thought and behaviour (leading to continued pursuit of dependent relations, even as they have been aware of its weaknesses[10]); and second, the related inability to come to terms with.

Table 3

**Share of Selected Sectors
in Target & Actual Investment**

(% of total allocation)

	Fifth Plan		Sixth Plan		7th Plan
	Target	Actual	Target	Actual	Target
Agriculture					
Public	10.1	10.0	4.7	7.1	4.5
Private	17.8	27.5	22.7	21.9	17.2
Total	12.4	16.0	12.1	3.1	9.7
Industry					
Public	15.5	16.3	8.6	6.2	4.6
Private	31.5	24.5	31.0	33.0	29.9
Total	20.2	19.1	17.7	17.1	15.0
Construction					
Public	6.6	6.1	4.7	10.0	5.7
Private	21.3	23.6	21.8	22.7	21.8
Total	10.9	12.2	11.7	15.2	12.3
Transport & Communications					
Public	18.5	21.9	17.4	18.6	17.6
Private	17.9	10.9	13.0	11.6	11.5
Total	18.3	18.1	15.6	15.8	15.1
Energy					
Public	*	*	27.2	21.8	25.8
Private	*	*	-	-	9.9
Total	*	*	16.1	13.0	19.2

#Mining and Manufacturing.   * not available.
##Physical Planning & Housing.   - nil or negligible.
Source: Planning & Development Division.

indigenous thoughts, traditions, and social classes, who stand to gain at the expense of the presently powerful classes, in any successful scheme of self-reliant development.

The suggestion in this monograph that the process of planning in Pakistan involves a bit of charlatanism is also not new. Mahbubul Haq [1968] had painted a fairly accurate picture, which remains valid:

> In the late 1940s, there arose a new priesthood of development planners—men who had tremendous confidence in themselves and little confidence in their societies which they wished to transform in a hurry.
>
> They promised every man a Chevrolet, or at least a Honda [in 1968, this referred to a motorcycle!], and then found that they could fulfil this promise only for themselves and for a privileged few.
>
> They were generally men of good intentions, often products of Western liberal education, who played the game of development with deadly seriousness.

But, as the proverb goes, the road to Hell is paved with bricks of good intention. In seeking to avoid that road, therefore, it is necessary to place confidence in our society, and in our traditions. Unfortunately, a Western liberal education provides the worst background for an assessment of our traditions. Before addressing the question of an appropriate development strategy for Pakistan, therefore, it is necessary to digress and discuss briefly the problems and possibilities that are a heritage of our geopolitical circumstances, history and traditions.

Chapter 4

ISLAMICATE[1] TRADITION AND POST-COLONIAL SOCIAL STRUCTURE

Pakistan is located at the eastern end of a unified region, from the Nile in Egypt to the Amu-Syr basin in Soviet Central Asia and from Anatolia in Turkey to the Indo-Gangetic plains. This region, the Muslim Heartland, has been the centre of human civilization and the main theatre of the rise of Islam. Today, in proximity to Pakistan, this region is bounded by India and Bangladesh on the east, Afghanistan and Soviet Turkmenistan, Uzbekistan, Tajikistan, Kazakhstan, and Kirgiziya to the north (all being 50-85% Muslim; the great majority, *Ḥanafī*), Iran and Turkey to the west, and the countries of the Arabian peninsula and Egypt to the southwest.

From a historical point of view, the unified history of this region, may be seen to fall in six periods [see p. 38].[2] Despite the vicissitudes of recent history (the last two hundred years), in which (among other things) national boundaries have changed, the people of this region still share a common Islamicate heritage and culture, with all its attendant strengths and problems. In any assessment of national security, as well as development strategy, it is essential to keep this framework in mind. Accordingly, we will review very briefly this heritage, the common problems which arise from it, and the specific circumstances which affect Pakistan, before addressing the question of how a development strategy can be devised to strengthen national security.

The Islamicate Tradition

The Islamicate tradition, common to this Nile-to-Oxus region, including Pakistan, consists of a rich variety of common developments which affect the Muslim *ummah* resident in the states which divide the region today. Four aspects of this tradition are of relevance to our discussion:

(i)   First, the nature of Islam, as a *dīn*, with its distinctive conception of human liberty through submission to Allah, a conception radically different from the prevailing modern [European] conception of human liberty based on material possessions.[4]

(ii)   Second, as a direct consequence of this world view, the historically powerful vision of the sharı ah as the only source of legitimacy and social order a vision which conflicts directly with the modern [European] conception of a secular rational order

SIX PERIODS IN MUSLIM HISTORY

485-692   Late Sasani and Early Caliphate[32]

Introduction of Islam into an Irano-Semitic society and the genesis of a new social order.

[Pakistan: Pre-Islamic period.]

692-945   High Caliphal Period

A classical Islamic civilization under the later Umayyads (Marwaani) and earlier Abbasid caliphates.

[Pakistan: The First Wave--Umayyads, invading from sea and over land, establish Muslim rule in Sind and Southwestern Punjab(711-714). Brahmanabad Settlement, 713; Ismaili state in Multan (977-1005) and Mansura (ca. 985-1025); Hindus re-established at Rohri (ca. 850s).]

945-1258   Earlier Middle Islamic Period

Establishment of an international civilization spreading beyond the Irano-Semitic area.

[Pakistan: The Second Wave--Afghan Turks, salves of the Samaanids of Bukhara (874-999), establish the Yamini dynasty of Ghazni (962), and invade across the northwestern passage to take Peshawar (ca. 1001) and Lahore (ca. 1020). Mahmud of Ghaznah (998-1030); after 1001, Ghaznavids also control the Punjab. Ghaznavids (1161-86), Ghurids (1186-1206), take Delhi (1193).]

1258-1503   Later Middle Islamic Period

The Age of Monogol Prestige: Crisis, assimilation and renewal in Islamicate institutions and heritage.

[Pakistan: Delhi Sultanate (1206-1526)--"Slave Kings" (1205-87), Khiljis (1290-1320), Tughlaqs (1320-51, expansion; 1351-1413, restricted to Northern India), Sayyids (1414-52), and Lodhis (1451-1526). Timur-Lang sacks Delhi, 1398.]

1503-1789   Earlier Modern Islamic Period

Flowering of Persianate culture under major regional empires.

[Pakistan: The Third Wave-Chughtai Turks, mistakenly called, Mughals (1526-1707); the "Twilight" of the Mughals (1707-1857). Nadir Shah sacks Delhi, 1739.]

1789-   Later Modern Islamic Period

The Age of European Prestige: Crisis and response.

[Pakistan: British hegemony (1798-1857) and colonialism (1857-1947); Independent Pakistan (since 1947). British occupy Indus Basin (1843-49); anti-British uprising, 1857; Khilaafat movement, 1919-24; Mohammad Ali Jinnah assumes leadership of Muslim League, 1936; secession of East Pakistan, 1971.]

conflicts directly with the modern [European] conception
of a secular rational order based on human laws.

(iii)   Third, historically, the commitment to
human liberty and to the *sharī'ah* led directly
to the formation of a 'shurafa'-'umara'
system of social power and authority, which
has survived to this day, in which social
power evolved not into corporate consensual
forms [in fact, municipal, local and central
power, often based on race, geography and
the exclusion of foreigners, was diminished],
but was shared by military commanders
('umara') and notables (*shurafā'*) in cities
[merchants] and villages [landowners].

(iv)   Finally, with the Mongol conquests, the
shurafā'- umara' system was transformed into
a military-patronage state, which has
provided the bases of modern absolutisms,
in which the steppe principles of nomad
patronage of citied culture were generalized
to the evolution of states as essentially
military constructs.

Islam: Liberty Under God   To be a Muslim is to
be a free person. This commitment to individual liberty
is embodied in *lā ilāha* (there is no divinity) and is
qualified only by *illa Allāh* (except Allah): thus, liberty
is distinguished from license, and submission to God is

to be both total and without any competing loyalties whatsoever: of church, or state, or tribe, or family, or spouse, or child, or wealth, or property.

The act of accepting Islam is therefore a compact between each Muslim as an individual and God, without any intermediaries; a compact to submit to Allah, in the manner exemplified by the Holy Prophet (ṣ.[5]) and to submit to no one else—except, as ordained by Him—in return for His promise of the bounties of Heaven (and earth).

Individual liberty, under the *sharīʿah*, then, is the very essence of Islam. It is the duty of each Muslim to find out what the *sharīʿah* asks of him or her, in each situation. Where he or she cannot personally do so, a community of scholars, the *'ulamā'*, are available to clarify points of the *sharīʿah*. The *'ulamā'* have no religious rights—they do not constitute a priesthood; there is no act of worship (usually mistranslated, ritual) in Islam which cannot be performed by the ordinary Muslim. It is incumbent upon each Muslim to benefit from their learning, and on them to respond to such requests.

Moreover, this *shahādah* (testimony) that 'There is no divinity except Allah, and Muḥammad (Ṣalla Allāh 'Alayhi wa sallam) is His Prophet' is sufficient to become a Muslim. The result is far-reaching: each Muslim is personally bound by this shahādah to discharge his or her responsibilities to Allah (*ḥuqūq*

Allāh), and to the community (*ḥuqūqul 'ibād*); each individual has certain personal obligations (*farḍ 'ayn*) and each community certain collective obligations (*farḍ kifāyah*). As a result, there is no distinction between private and public law; in particular, no individual can forego his personal responsibility before God to command the right and forbid the wrong, by sub-contracting the maintenance of order to limited groups in society.

Historically, in the last fourteen hundred years, where this radical conception of human liberty has provided the opportunity to individual Muslims to lead lives of unmatched freedom and dignity, it has also raised fundamental problems for the Muslim community in the imposition of social order.[5] These problems persist to this day, but our appreciation of these problems and their remedies are determined to a large extent by the views of European scholars, who have understandably viewed themselves as the centre of the universe and history (Eurocentricism), and have not had a chance to benefit from God's guidance (*hidāyah*) or the experience of Islam.

This conception of man's predicament on earth and the challenge of the act of being Muslim, is held closely by the educated elite who are the bearers of indigenous high culture, and enjoys a degree of respect and esteem, well in excess of a precise understanding in these terms, among the vast majority of the people of Pakistan–both at the level of 'folk culture' and among the custodians of the rival high culture, the modernizing elite. This is not without consequence in modern efforts to impose an alien scheme of social, political, and economic order in an effort to 'harness' social energies for increased production for acquisition and consumption of goods, as a source of furthering human liberty.

Authority and Law: The Sharʿī Vision   When the Prophet (ṣ.) was alive, all authority, moral and temporal, was embodied in his person. Despite serious differences in the community, this situation continued in the times of the *al-khulafā' al-rāshidūn*. In subsequent generations, however, a split occurred between the sources of moral authority in the community (the *'ulamā'*) and the sources of coercive power and patronage (the *umarā'*, or military commanders, who were the rulers), with far-reaching consequences for the community to this day. A vision of the community based on the *sharīʿah*, nevertheless, continued to develop among the *'ulamā'*, and remained popular in the Muslim community at large.

The system of authority and law, envisaged in this *sharʿī* vision, was based on three principles:

(i)   First, the basis for law was to be neither deduction from abstract principles nor legislation by a human assembly, but the empirical observation of individual actions which were demonstrably approved by God[6]-on the basis of *Qur'ān, ḥadīth, ijmā'*, and *qiyās* ('ilm being the knowledge of the process of demonstrating the approval of Allah);[7]

(ii)   Second, the basis for organization within the community was to be twofold: *farḍ 'ayn* or duties which everyone is obligated to, whether others perform them or not (such as worship or keeping one's contracts); and *farḍ kifāyah* or duties inherently incumbent upon all members of the community, but which could be left aside by some as long as some other person or persons in the community discharged the responsibility–from this it follows that there need not be any constitution, nor any separate public law, as legally all public duties were to be discharged on almost the same basis as private ones; and

(iii)   Finally, a basis for toleration of dissent from Islam itself was established in the establishment of the rights and obligations of the *dhimmīs* or the 'protected subjects' of a Muslim community.

This is not the place to get into a detailed discussion of the virtues of the *sharī'ah*. Suffice it to note that it was the basis, historically, of a social order in which individual justice, and an individualistic egalitarianism, was promoted at the expense of vague notions of social justice and collective interest. The criminal law was mild by comparison to the times; procedure was quick; money fines, which discriminate against the poor, were rare. Unlike Jewish, Christian or any other practice at the time (or even now), the Muslim woman's property could not legally be touched by her husband. There was no primogeniture: one son was not preferred over the other. By Abbasid times, the personal dignity of Muslims and their demand for quick and speedy justice was met by a system of qadi courts, the *muhtasib* (market inspector) who got his law from the *qāḍī*, and the *shurṭah* (police force) which ensured compliance of the *muhtasib*'s orders.

This system of law and authority, modelled on the life of the Muslim community at Medina (622-632), developed in the times of the *al-khulafā' al-rāshidūn* (632-661) and the Umayyads (661-750) and perfected in Abbasid times (750-1258), served the Muslim community handsomely, throughout the Nile-to-Oxus region, for some one thousand years. Despite the doctrinal differences which arose, partly in response to the reconstitution of society and authority in the wake of the Mongol invasions, the system retained a remarkable uniformity in its development—whether in the Safavi (1503-1722), the

Ottoman (1517-1718), or the Mughal empire (1526-1707).

It was the rise of high-consumption societies in Europe in the nineteenth century, and the consequent colonization of much of these lands, which served to disrupt the unity of Muslim law and moral authority. With the passage of colonialism, the bulk of the population retains a latent sympathy toward this vision of a *sharī* community, which holds a powerful sway over the hearts and minds of the vernacular elite of these Muslim lands: the *'ulamā'*, the *mashā'ikh*,[8] and sympathetic vernacular intellectuals.

Evolution of the Social Order   This conception of human liberty, bounded only by the *sharī'ah*, has led throughout history to two patterns in the evolution of the social order: first, a persistent difficulty in forming any kind of intermediate bureaucratic structure, and local and central authority on the basis of popular consent; and second, the consequent tendency toward militarization of social power.[9] Islamicate society, based as it was on the insistence of the individual to confront God face to face, with the minimum of intermediaries, naturally demanded a social order of much greater openness than was to evolve either in the feudal societies of Europe to the West, or in the caste-based society of India to the East, or in the structured bureaucratic rank-based society of China in North-East.

In the Hijaz, Islamicate society was a society of city merchants, dominating a nomadic surrounding.[10] With the expansion of Islam societies based on agrarian power (in the major river valleys) were subdued. Initially, social and political power shifted to the encampments of the conquering military commanders (the *umarā'*), under whose patronage the activities of Muslim merchants tilted the balance of social power in favour of urban-mercantile elements. Soon, however, a monarchy was reconstituted, as the *amīr* gradually became *sulṭān*, and agrarian interests resumed their upper hand. In this reconstitution, however, older social structures were remoulded along more open, egalitarian, contractual, bases, in which appeal was made to the *sharī'ah* rather than to the pre-Islamic custom for ultimate legitimacy.

These developments, together with objective factors (sparseness of concentrated agricultural holdings and pastoral competition, in an era of booming long-distance commerce), led to a stalemate between the landed families and city merchants, neither of whom was able to establish domoninance over the other. Thus, to put it in later European categories, neither bourgeoisie nor gentry, could act in independence. The consequent stalemate in finding common institutions to legitimize the power of landed families in the countryside and the local autonomy of commercial cities, led to a vacuum in which militarized governments moved with rare ease.

The resulting social system functioned by way of such things as: the *shari'ah* law; at the base of power a free peasantry under military land grants *(iqta');* the patronage of the *shurafa'* (notables] of the towns; succession by appointment or contest; the slave household; and, at the centre of power, the *amir's* garrison courts; all these presupposing and supporting each other. This system of social power can be called the *shurafa' umara'* system (as an ideal type, only approximated in reality]: in which power is divided between notables in cities and countryside, and commanders of local garrisons, with minimal interference from large-scale political organizations.[11]

This pattern of society came to Sind and Southwestern Punjab in the first wave of Islamic expansion in Pakistan (starting 711-713), and has had a lasting impact on social structures, despite modifications entailed in the two successive waves of conquest—first by the Turkic Mongols (starting ca. 1000) and then by the British (starting ca. 1843-49)—which were not without impact on social structures. The social impact, however, of Turkish and British conquests is best considered in the context of the evolution of the political order.

Evolution of the Political Order Before the Mongol irruption, all efforts at state formation took place in the persistent backdrop of the distribution of power between the *shurafa'* and the *umara'* in the towns. The forms of government which arose in Islamicate societies as a result proceeded first, with Arab rule, from government by an egalitarian privileged people *en bloc*, to the emergence of Persian ways, in which government was by a neutral absolute monarch on the pattern of the Sasanid empire which was absorbed, to the emergence of Turkic government by a privileged military family, along with a privileged people as almost an extension of that family, through its patronage. But these patterns were not racial; they had a logic of their own in the evolution of the social order along the *shurafā'- umarā'* system, which made society especially susceptible to militarization of political power. (Hodgson 1974, 2:409).

Unlike the Hijaz, where the symbiosis of city and desert was on the terms of the city, in the steppe of Central Asia the Mongol nomad held the upper hand over the cities. The Turkic warrior horsemen, with their sheep and goat herds, and complex camp apparatus required to provide them with mobility, carried a strategic advantage over the settled citied-agrarianate society lacking structure and organization. At the same time, it provided the bases of militarization of government, in isolation from civilian population. The Mongol state formations, not unexpectedly, were therefore essentially military constructs.

Out of these constructs grew the military-patronage state, in which: first, the dynastic law of the ruling family (the Yasa), independent of the *sharīʿah* and customary law *(ʿādah)* was recognized as legitimate, allowing rule by decree; second, the whole state was conceived as a single military force, with the civilian bureaucracy being absorbed into the military; and third, all privilege and responsibility was distributed among members of a military family, served by a class of notables who enjoyed the patronage of the rulers and were almost an extension of the military family—all the rest were merely *riʿāyah* ('herds'), who were to be protected and taxed (milked).

It was the Turkic tradition, informed by Persian sensibilities then current, which above all fashioned social and political institutions in the Delhi Sultanate and the Mughal empire, which are our heritage in Pakistan. The basic conception of the state, its administrative apparatus, and its social mores were not reconstituted in any radical way by the British. The impact of British hegemony and colonialism, however, had a profound impact in that the British, unlike the Turkic rulers, projected their power from settled agrarian societies, in which they retained their original cultures, and were not assimilated within Islam—even though the early colonials did assimilate Islamicate ways. The twist given to this Islamicate tradition, and the modes of reaction, are of current interest.

The Colonial Experience and Reaction

Starting with the French Revolution, in 1789, the Europeans started on a two hundred year path of establishing a high-consumption social order, which necessarily entailed the colonization of the bulk of the non-European world (from about 1875 to 1914; a state of affairs which prevailed until the late 1950s), including the Nile-to-Oxus area. The ability of the Europeans to do this, although not central to our argument, arose both from their mastery of superior military doctrine and technology, and to the breakdown of Islamicate societies internally, through a growing fondness for luxury inspired by the rise of earlier imperial Iranian patterns, and externally, by the irruption of the Turkic-Mongol tribes, which can be dated from the sacking of Baghdad in 1258 and Delhi in 1398, who swept into this region and subsequently accepted Islam.

The most significant result of the colonial experience was the havoc it wreaked on the Muslim psyche, moral framework, and culture; not, as scholarship in the Europeanate tradition would have it, on the economies of the region—although the plunder was certainly there. In addition, as part of colonial policy, the European powers gave rise to a mutation in Islamicate society, a social class, imbued with both a powerful sense of its own worth and an Evangelical-Utilitarian perspective on society, politics and economy.[12] To this

day this class holds all power and is the greatest impediment to sustainable social change.

The reaction to European colonialism was both
immediate and widespread throughout the Nile-to-Oxus
region. Also, there was considerable uniformity in the
approach that evolved throughout the Muslim Heartlan-
d.[13] In the British Indian colony, after the suppression
of the uprising against the British in 1857, three centres
of   Muslim   national   leadership   emerged   in
British-colonized India: Deoband, Aligarh and Nadwah.
Although these names are associated with three
institutions of learning, still extant in India, the men
associated with them symbolized three distinct
ideological approaches to the reform of Islamicate
society in the face of the threat of European cultural
dominance.

(i)   *Conservative Orthodoxy (Deoband)*   The
          conservative reaction was representative by
          the class of *'ulamā'* associated with the
          founding of the seminary at Deoband in
          1866, with the purpose of re-establishing
          contact between the *'ālim* and the average
          Muslim, and to reorient the Muslim com-
          munity to its original cultural and religious
          identity.[14]

(ii)   *Reactive-Modernism (Aligarh)*   The task set
          by the founder of Aligarh (1875), Sir Sayyid
          Ahmad Khan (1817-98), who had fought

alongside the British in 1857, was slightly different: to incorporate Islam within an uncompromisingly modern outlook. Sir Sayyid, a controversial personality because of his personal beliefs, advocated the almost uncritical acceptance of Western civilization and its materialist basis, while rejecting those aspects of Islam and the *Qur'ān* which could not be verified by the senses or experience, so as to evolve an Islam compatible with the scientific standards of late nineteenth century Europe. In time, however, enlightened Muslim opinion rallied around his efforts to educate Muslims for the modern world, which came in time to be identified in Pakistan as the one most favourable to modernization and development.

(iii)   *Conservative-Modernism (Nadwah)*   In an attempt to bridge the bitter rivalry between Deoband and 'Aligarh, in 1893, *Nadwat al-'ulamā'* was founded to serve as a bridge between Islamic and Western culture, and the orthodox *'ulamā'* and the modernists, and to arrive at a balanced synthesis of the best of the old and the new.

Unlike Aligarh, which sought modernism constrained by Islam, Nadwah sought Islam within constraints of modernity; but its efforts were met by hostility from both sides. The failure of Nadwah was the failure to find common ground between orthodoxy and modernism; to incorporate a modern outlook within Islam; and was symptomatic of problems which have plagued us to this day.

Post-Colonial Social Structure

In all post-colonial nations, the most fundamental division—in values, morals, opinions, intellect, habits, and lifestyles—lies between two classes, which may be called the vernacular class (the class that does not speak English, who correspond to the ri'āyah, but now include the vernacular soldier—the jawān) and, in our context, the anglophile class (the class that speaks English, who are the shurafā' and umarā' combined).[15] Because of its novelty, thinking in terms of vernacular-anglophile takes getting used to. Over time, the anglophile class has also become stratified. Thus one can speak of the anglophile elite as well as anglophile middle and lower classes (or even, proletariat). In this taxonomy, for example, the major religious political parties (like the Jamā'at-i-Islāmī), would be seen to be led by and consist largely of anglophiles (although they may also have many vernacular workers), the urban office worker, the lower (but not the lowest) level local government functionary, all would be seen to be anglophile, as would be the small trader; and so on.

The internal distribution of power between the vernacular and the anglophile class may be explored in terms of the instruments of power identified above–authority, patronage, and coercive ability. Finally, these instruments may be located concretely, to clarify the concept even further.

Authority   For the vernacular class, authority tends to reside in the *'ulamā'-mashā'ikh*–whose symbols are the *Qur'ān* and the *sunnah,* or the *sharī'ah;* for the anglophile class, in the progressive intellectual–whose symbols are science-technology, constitutional democracy (whether socialist or capitalist), and modern (by which is meant, Europeanate) laws. (This is, of course, a general tendency; in specific situations, especially during major national struggles against alien powers, the personal character of individual leaders have prevailed over normal class loyalties.)

Patronage   In the vernacular class, patronage lies almost exclusively in private wealth: in traders, merchants, and a few landlords, whose very wealth enables their second and third generations (who are so inclined; and the bulk are) to make the transition to the anglophile class–the *waqf,* traditionally the major source of patronage by and for the vernacular class, having been brought under the firm control of the anglophile class since the days of President Ayub Khan. In the anglophile class, private wealth is to be found in land, commerce and industry, while the much greater scope for patronage arises from a firm control of government, politics and statecraft, and especially of the civil and military bureaucracy.

Coercive Power Coercive power is held firmly in the hands of the anglophile class, in the civil and military bureaucracy, to which induction is regulated by the Public Service Commissions and the Inter-Services Selection Board. Both ensure that the candidates selected are already from the anglophile class or possess the potential and inclination to be groomed into an anglophile orientation. The vernacular class, strictly speaking, has only one route to wielding coercive power: through elections. It is for this reason that candidates selected by the Election Commission (even though itself in the hands of the anglophile class) have never had much of a chance against candidates selected by the Service Commissions and Board.

The Location of Power The location of these three aspects of power, in our context, are the mosques and the universities (where primarily symbolic power is exercised, in their respective spheres); the bazars-markets (where the secretariats and the thanas are represented in subtle and not so subtle ways); and the secretariats, thanas and the general headquarters (GHQ). There is, of course, no one-to-one relation between the instruments of power (authority, patronage, and coercion), its sources (symbols, property, and organization), and its location (secretariat and mosque, bazar-market, thana-GHQ). In specific circumstances, these aspects will all tend to overlap; nevertheless, it is useful to distinguish the primary components.

With this perspective, it should be clear for example that the quest for establishment of democratic institutions is the quest of political government to win the respect of the progressive intellectuals, *'ulamā',* and *mashā'ikh;* to wrench patronage from the hands of the bureaucracy; and to establish control over the coercive powers of the thana and the GHQ. In terms of power, this framework provides a useful frame of reference for the analysis of many other important social and political issues.

Implications for National Solidarity

As a result of this internal structure, one of the major problems we face, in common with other Muslim countries, is the diffusion of power among competing social groups. In moral and spiritual matters, the *'ulamā'* and the *mashā'ikh* still command the undivided loyalty of the bulk of the people. In temporal matters, coercive authority is seen to reside clearly with the military and civil bureaucracy. Political leadership, therefore, motivated mainly by the power of patronage, is burdened with a constant struggle for legitimacy. Unlike European countries, in the popular perception no moral legitimacy have seldom been able to control the bureaucracy. This is the genesis of the problem of political stability.

This diffusion of power between the 'ulamā'-mashā'ikh, the military-bureaucracy, and the political government (legislature-executive) is of important and far-reaching consequences for the internal dynamics of society. These are not, however, the main subjects of this monograph. In terms of national security, the question of power relates to the exercise of these powers vis-a-vis other nations and the ability to resist similar action by other nations. Any strategy for enhancing security must consist of three components: military, diplomatic and economic. As the first two are not the subjects of this monograph, we conclude with the broad features of an approach to development strategy which would enhance security.

Chapter 5

TOWARDS AN INTEGRATED STRATEGY

In the context of our geopolitical and historical heritage, the question of an appropriate strategy to promote national security and economic development can now be addressed. Obviously, a complete blueprint can only be evolved through a process of social dialogue, involving all elements, over an extended period. Nevertheless, an outline of an approach towards the evolution of the elements of such a strategy could be identified as follows:

(i)   *Establishment of a primum mobile*: Before there can be strategy, there must be a strategist. It is essential, therefore, to establish a group at the highest level of the state, which would command the compliance of the civil and military bureaucracy, and would formulate and monitor the implementation of a grand strategy. This could either be a National Security Agency, or a radically restructured Planning Commission, or a separate body which is invested with the prestige and authority needed to render its functioning effective, and is so structured as to shelter it from the vagaries of party politics so that it can serve the wider and long-term interests of Pakistan.

(ii) *Agreement on common ground*: In order to create a strategic consensus, the objectives (at least to begin with) must be confined to those specified in the Constitution.

(iii) *Consolidation of authority*: The first element of the grand strategy would be to create a consensus around a conception of authority, as embodied in the Constitution, namely:

- **Islam**: in its total cultural aspect (where culture means *dīn*), to be established by a systematic well-thought out policy on dissemination of information, and on education (including the establishment of a pluralist, Islamicate, literate culture based on the national language, supported by regional languages and sub-cultures); and

- **Justice**: provided through a uniform system of law, justice, and police, which assures that agreement on authority is translated into outcomes that are not only just, but are seen to be so.

(iv) *Restructuring the patronage system*: The second element of the strategy would be to restrict the enormous patronage presently extended by foreign (and domestic) groups hostile to, or working at cross-purposes from, the conception of authority, reflecting national Islamic values as envisaged in the Constitution, which is to be created. In addition, a system should be established in which the conferment of benefits upon private parties is done openly, by elected representatives of the people, at the local, provincial and federal level, rather than behind closed doors by the bureaucracy. This would involve a fundamental revision of the institutional framework of policy-making, and of economic policies, which should be designed to foster self-reliant growth.

(v)   *Resisting coercive power*: The third element of the strategy would be to seek innovative ways to meet the prospect of an adverse military balance for some time to come. Two suggestions would be to implement a strategic population settlement programme on the right bank of the Indus (to lend defensive depth), and to formulate and implement a new strategic doctrine. In addition, very high qualities of statesmanship would be called for to create opportunities where normal bureaucratic responses would not be adequate.

The Primum Mobile

Before outlining an integrated strategy, we should be clear who should implement this strategy. Although all classes in society attempt to alter the course of development within the means at their command, it should be clear from what has been said above that it is primarily the civil and military bureaucracy which plays a decisive role in shaping development strategy. Today the bureaucracy, however, is itself an assortment of individuals with differing abilities and inclinations, and is too large and diffused to be an effective instrument of strategy formulation.

Moreover, under the present arrangements, the task for designing a development strategy falls largely to the Planning and Development Division, under the guidance of the Planning Commission (which has not really functioned since the late 1960s) and the National Economic Council, which lacks a homogeneity of interests and outlook. In order to be effective, in order to conceive of development (and security) in the largest perspective, it is essential to broaden the base of planning.

Accordingly, consideration must be given to the establishment of a Commission of the highest standing (like a National Security Agency, or a radically different Planning Commission) or a separate high powered body, staffed not by bureaucrats, or politicians, but by suitable professionals of stature, assisted by experts in the diplomatic, economic, and military fields.[1]

An effective strategy for security and development must be designed and implemented by a more broad-based, as well as more homogeneous body. To be successful, the task must be seen as the joint task of the civil and military bureaucracy, acting in cohesion and with purpose. This will not be easy to accomplish; nor will it come about immediately.

Agreement on Common Ground: The Constitution

The first task of any strategy for promoting national security and economic development must be to foster a much more cohesive sense of nationhood than exists at present. Common citizens must feel that there is something worthwhile to defend and develop, before there can be any defence or development. If it is felt that those in positions of authority rob whenever they can and pay only when they must, if it is felt that injustice is the order of the day, and that the law is an instrument of tyranny, then it would be natural for the people to feel alienated from the nation. In the presence of this sense of alienation, no amount of armaments, no amount of foreign assistance, no plan for economic development will succeed.

This much is widely recognized. From here, however, the road divides along the cognitive class lines which we have inherited from our colonial history: the preponderant, but weak, vernacular class expects that the nation will be integrated around Islam and tradition; the anglophile class believes that the inherent moral superiority of modernization goals justify the adoption of any means to transform the nation into a rational, secular, scientific, modern state–in the image of the West. As has been pointed out there is no middle ground; nor motive, willingness or effort to seek common ground.

How is this cleavage to be bridged? I would suggest that as a strategy we declare a moratorium on discussions of doctrine. As an intermediate stage, let us abide by the Constitution, and implement those values which are implicit in this most imperfect of documents, which has the sole virtue of being the only statement of agreed principles. In order for this tactic to work, all must do so in good faith. We must recognise the gravity of the present moment in our history, and abandoning all reservations–however valid they may be–realizing the grave dangers of discord, unite behind the Constitution.

In time, once the nation has achieved a degree of cohesion and strength, we may well be able to take up, and we must, the debate on larger questions of doctrine. Surprisingly, of the two classes, the vernacular class would be more easily persuaded of this. It is the anglophile class, despite its profession of modern values, which is the first to undermine the Constitution: it somehow believes that the Constitution is a compromised, imperfect document, itself a strategic construct in the quest for modernity, which should not therefore be taken too seriously if it stands in the way of the achievement of larger modernization goals. This attitude is self-defeating.

Consensus on Authority: On 'Constitutional' Islam

From its historic role of being the source of unity for the Muslim *ummah,* Islam today has become a bone of contention between the anglophile class, which has inherited the mantle of colonial power in the post-colonial era, and the large majority of Muslims who continue to lead their lives in Islamicate if not Islamic ways. This is not difficult to understand, if we keep in mind the history of the colonial experience and the variety of nationalist response.

The Shari Vision   As the earlier discussion of the Islamicate heritage has pointed out, however, the commitment to the *shari* vision and to associated cultural norms is widespread, and can be ignored only at great cost. Without a doubt, the single most important choice which confronts our statesmen, and statesmen of Islamicate states in general, is whether to channel national energies to the attainment of this vision, or to attempt to ignore, manipulate or subvert this vision. In particular, whether to make of Islam what Europeanate civilization has made of Christianity, a benevolent superstition and a private social phenomenon, carefully excluded from law, politics and the norms of public conduct.

No matter what the decision, a way must be found to accommodate the popular *shari* vision with the modernization goals of the anglophile class. The Constitution (despite its many limitations, admittedly) is itself the product of the anglophile class and hence is closer to their goals; it is therefore perhaps the best document which can serve as a source of common ground. Under the Constitution, it is incumbent upon the state, inter alia, to:[2]

Establish an order, wherein Muslims shall be enabled to order their lives in the individual and collective spheres in accordance with the teachings and requirements of Islam as set out in the Holy *Qur'ān* and *Sunnah*. (Preamble; see also, under Principles of Policy, Article 31(1).[3]

Make the teaching of the Holy *Qur'ān* and Islamiyat compulsory, to encourage and facilitate the learning of Arabic language; to promote unity and the observance of Islamic moral standards; and to secure the proper organization of *zakāt, 'ushr, awqāf* and mosques. (Under Principles of Policy, Article 31(2).)

Prevent prostitution, gambling and taking of injurious drugs; prevent the consumption of alcoholic liquor; eliminate *ribā* as early as possible; and endeavour to preserve and strengthen fraternal relations among Muslim countries based on Islamic unity. (Under Principles of Policy, Articles 37(g)(h), 38(f), and 40.)

In addition, the Constitution provides for a Federal Shariat Court which, notwithstanding anything contained in the Constitution, is empowered to examine and decide whether any law is un-Islamic (excluding the

Constitution, Muslim personal law, or any law of procedure; and until 24th June 1990, any fiscal or financial law). Where the Shariat Court finds any law un-Islamic, the matter can be brought before the Supreme Court in appeal, and if the Court upholds the decision of the Shariat Court, the law ceases to have effect and it becomes incumbent upon the President to amend the law in question.[4]

Finally, the Constitution requires that all existing laws be brought in conformity with the injunctions of Islam as laid down in the *Qur'ān* and *Sunnah* (Art. 227). To do so, it provides for the constitution of a Council of Islamic Ideology (Art. 228), to consider references and give advice to the President, Governors and the Assemblies on whether proposed laws are Islamic, and to compile for their benefit, *suo moto*, such Islamic laws as can be given legislative effect (Arts. 229, 230(b)(f)); and to make recommendations to them on how Muslims can be enabled to order their lives in accordance with Islam, and how laws can be brought into conformity with Islam.

These provisions have not been implemented in good faith. The bureaucracy, given its anglophile cultural orientation, has not lived up to even these weak commitments to Islam embodied in the Constitution. Apart from its impact on Islamization, this has served to undermine respect for the 'Rule of Law' which is so cherished a goal of modernization. It is essential that this situation be corrected immediately, and tactical delays be avoided.

Culture, Islam and Ethnicity   A central lesson of Islamic history is that the Muslim community is much easier parted from power and wealth than from its culture (*dīn*). Whenever rulers have sought to interfere with the cultural behaviour of the governed, they have suffered grave consequences. It is Islamicate culture which is threatened today by the path of development chosen by the anglophile elite of Pakistan. There is, however, widespread concern at social unrest and ethnic strife. This is attributed either to domestic causes (a favourite being a rise in ethnicity at the expense of Islam, as a source of identity) or to foreign ones (essentially, subversion and insurgency).

The key to understanding ethnic strife, however, lies in understanding strife not ethnicity.[5] I do not believe that what we are observing reflects any structural social change—in the sense either of a rise of ethnic-nationalism en route to a rise of class consciousness (in keeping with Marxist dogma[6]) or of a transition from a tribal to ethnolinguistic self-image (in line with 'American' social science dogma.[7] These views reflect the inability of Europeanate scholars, not surprisingly given their history, to conceive of nationhood on anything higher than race or geography. The most obvious alternative explanation for the situation would lie in the structure of distribution of access to public services, jobs and patronage, on the basis of domicile and location.

Islam and Islamicate culture are very much a force today in Pakistan. Within the vernacular class, ethnicity has seldom posed any problem. Unfortunately, the division of spoils within the anglophile class is structured along lines which exacerbate a sense of ethnic injustice. The root of the evil can be traced to the manner in which the intent of the Constitution has been subverted. The Constitution forbids discrimination on non-merit grounds, but provides for special allowances being made for disadvantaged groups. For example:

- Under Art. 22(3)(b), it is forbidden to deny admission to any public educational institution on ground of place of birth; but, as a saving provision, under Art. 22(4) public authorities are allowed to make provisions for the advancement of backward classes of citizens.
- Under Art. 27(1), discrimination by place of birth in government appointments is forbidden, but a saving provision provides that for twenty years (extended from the initial ten) posts may be reserved for persons belonging to any class or area to secure their adequate representation.

In practice, however, in the guise of protecting the interests of the disadvantaged, quotas have been established for all classes, with the result that the disadvantaged have been precluded from access to most of the opportunities which have been available on a nationwide basis. This has naturally created provincial insularity and ethnic strife. The correct thing to do would be to define backward or minority classes on a nationwide basis (say the rural Sindhis, the Baluchis, and the Azad Kashmiris–who constitute less than 20 per cent of the population), and allow them to compete for all opportunities in all provinces and locations, in addition to opportunities reserved for them, while restricting eligibility of the stronger groups as necessary by local or provincial quotas.

In addition to domestic factors, there is no doubt that external factors are also at work in promoting social unrest, by exploiting whatever divisions they can create or foment.

The designs of our enemies are not only on our land and our wealth. It is Muslim culture (*dīn*) which has been (and is being) strongly opposed by the Indians, the Americans and the Soviets. It is not surprising therefore that after the most bitter conflict among the superpowers, today all are united that the post-Soviet government in Afghanistan should be non-Islamic, a view which finds silent sympathy among modern Muslims as well. Briefly, the proximate roots of this antipathy are as follows:

(i)   The Indian opposition to Muslim culture has three bases: first, the visceral Hindu distaste for the culture of what it views as outcastes; second, the Westernized Indian (Hindu and Muslim) view of Islam as a medieval antimodern outlook; and finally, the Indian nationalists' perception of the role of Muslim culture in reducing the vision of India in its moment of glory, at independence.

(ii)   The Soviet antipathy to Islam can be traced to three factors: first, Marxist-Leninist dogma which views religion as a reactionary force not compatible with advanced socialism; second, their view of Islam as a (i) foreign (Arab, Iranian, Ottoman) import into Soviet Central Asia, (ii) submissive to the Czarist regime, despite its anti-Russian character, (iii) conservative (even reactionary) and anti-social (sanctifying the authority of elders, humiliating women, inculcating fanaticism, intolerance and xenophobia), (iv) with primitive, barbarian and unhealthy rites (like circumcision and fasting), and (v) with a moral framework opposed to Communist morals; and finally, to their experience in Central Asia in which Soviet efforts to wipe out Islam–through genocide, massive transfers of population, anti-religious propaganda, implementation beginning in 1924 of the policy of *razmezhevanie* ('parcelling') of the Muslims of Central Asia into ethno-linguistic 'nations' with manufactured languages, cultures and even history, and since 1945 the two-stage policy of assimilation (first, 'getting nearer' *sblizhenie*, then 'merging' *sliyanie*), have all failed in destroying Muslim identity and culture, and enlisting them in the grand cause of creating a society based on advanced socialism (Bennigsen and Broxup 1983, pp. 46-47, 51-51, 135).

(iii)   The American antipathy to Islam, inherited to some extent from the British, three sources: first, as post-Christian cultures, they inherit the mind-set of the Crusades; second, they are perpetrators and victims of the elaborate intellectual structure built up over the last two hundred years in support of empire, and racist attitudes, called orientalism; and third, under the influence of the Zionists, they are active partisans in the Arab-Israeli conflict.

Common to all three is the assumption, based on their own histories, that people cannot be motivated by transcendent goals; that race and ethnicity are the highest objects of human allegiance and loyalty. The Indian naturally thinks of Hinduism, with its caste-based exclusive message, as the supreme expression of human values, and is unable to comprehend a message addressed to all humanity without bar of race or colour, which has the distinction of having been realised in history for extended periods. The Anglo-American is convinced that the rational-secular-materialist culture that Europe has erected on the ruins of Christianity is the best achievement of God or man, and despite its failure to absorb even the smallest of minorities of non-European racial extract, he is unable to comprehend the possibility of the moral superiority of a spiritual other-worldly outlook, especially as a viable basis for a universal human civilization. The Soviets are convinced of the moral superiority of Marxism-Leninism as the sole route to human salvation, and despite the severely repressive nature of the path they have chosen, they cannot accept the possibility of establishing a brotherhood of man in free submission to God, rather than in collective pursuit of goods and services.

This antipathy to Islam, combined with the affirmation of racist sentiments in their own experience, produces a response to Islam which comprehends the dynamics of Muslim society in terms of their own experience—race, ethnicity, economic motives, political dynamics. The Anglo-American, who has the comfort of a certain degree of isolation from Muslims, exhibits it in styles of scholarship. The Indians and Soviets, who live uncomfortably with large Muslim minorities, engage in promoting ethnicity as a policy of subversion and insurgency—often supported by innocent, and not so innocent, American scholarship.

The history of Soviet methods of promoting ethnicity among Muslims, to divide and then brutally suppress Central Asian Muslim communities is well-known (for details see Annexure). In a few words, however, Bennigsen and Wimbush (1979, p. 106) have described this strategy as follows:

Soviet strategy consistently has sought the destruction of pan-Turkic and pan-Islamic allegiances and movements in the Muslim regions of the USSR through the fragmentation of the Dar ul-Islam and the reconstitution of these people into separate and distinct nations. This strategy has included a massive expenditure on the reeducation of the affected peoples to think of themselves both ethnically and culturally in terms of smaller national units.

An awareness of the Soviet experience with its Muslim communities should serve to put concrete meaning on suspicions expressed frequently that external hands may also be active in the rise of ethno-linguistic nationalism in Pakistan. Given the Soviet experience, no doubt regarded by them as successful, and the Indian 'success' in engineering the secession of East Pakistan (with ethno-linguistic identity playing an important role) it would not be surprising if similar strategies may not be at work in Indo-Soviet efforts to de-stabilize Pakistan. The timing of the rise of ethnic organizations in Pakistan, in the wake of the Soviet invasion of Afghanistan in 1979, also does not seem fortuitous.

Urdu and the Language Question In the light of this discussion, we should also address the issue of Urdu as a national language. According to the 1981 Population Census, of those literate, 70 per cent are literate in

Urdu only; the proportion being fairly constant across all provinces. The opposition to Urdu, such as it is, comes largely from the English-educated classes. On the other hand, intellectuals of the vernacular class, of all provincial origins, seek actively to promote the use of Urdu.

According to press reports, on September 15, 1988, three identical privilege motions were discussed in the Senate, to the effect that the government had been remiss in not making arrangements for official use of the national language Urdu by August 14, 1988. The government responded that the 15 year period mentioned in the Constitution (which expired on August 14, 1988) was of a recommendatory nature and was not mandatory.

This opposition to Urdu is based on a misguided notion that the constitutional requirement of enforcing Urdu as a national language would lead either to a suppression of regional languages or of English, or both. Nothing could be farther from the truth. Ideally, the educated Pakistani would be fluent not only in his mother tongue but also in Urdu. In addition, Urdu would serve as a link language not only within the country, but as a medium of learning all other languages, including English. At present, there are very few Pakistanis who know any foreign language apart from English. Ideally, our universities and colleges should be teaching not only English, but French, German, Russian, Chinese, Japanese, as well as many of the less widely spoken languages. To learn these languages, it should not be necessary for all students to first learn English and then learn these languages. We must possess the capability to teach these languages from a common national language.

This language can be flexible, in which a free policy of assimilating from regional languages should be used in keeping with actual practice. But unless we develop the confidence of committing ourselves to the development of a national language, we cannot expect to take our place in the first rank of nations.

What is required is that support to Urdu should be given at the highest levels. For instance, to begin with, the government should demand that all Summaries for the Cabinet, Cabinet committees and sub-committees, and other high-powered bodies should be submitted in Urdu. This will automatically exert considerable pressure for the conduct of preparatory work at lower levels also in the Urdu language. The difficulty, it should be recognized, will be experienced mainly by our anglophile class leadership. This difficulty should be dealt with sympathetically, and in the initial period, translators should be allowed to high officials to assist them in the transition.

Information Policy There is a need to realise that the mass media are the most powerful sources of creating mental attitudes—of respect, love, loyalty, fear, greed--which go into creating national character, and its attributes, whether of independent self-confidence or of fearful dependence. It should be recalled that national security lies in our abilities as a nation to resist alien authority, patronage and coercion. In this the mass media play a powerful role.

The audio-visual media–particularly, television–being accessible to the literate and illiterate population alike, are the most powerful purveyors of symbols. They are like an intravenous line into the jugular of national consciousness. Having placed that line the greatest of care needs to be taken to insure that the images we feed in are those that strengthen national security and not weaken it. Similarly, newspapers, magazines and the like serve to mould public sentiment and opinions which are not neutral in their cultural content. Unfortunately, this fact is not fully appreciated.

When we show our children, young adults, and adults imported films and television programmes, we expose them not only to the plot of the story, but to the entire cultural context in which human emotions are screened. The common human virtues–of love, honour, duty and the like–portrayed in popular television programmes make a ready place in our heart; but the context also smuggles in the desire for an American kitchen, a large car, styles of living room furniture, and of relating to friends, in-laws, and family, not to mention those aspects of lifestyle which the Constitution would call 'repugnant' to Islam. This place which is created in the hearts of the audience is at the expense of our own culture and values.

The same is true about written matter. At the highest levels of government, matters of high statesmanship are decided on the basis of attitudes and opinions formed by *Readers' Digest, Time, Newsweek, Economist, Foreign Affairs*, and the like. It is not surprising then that Prime Minister Mr. H. S. Suhrawardy was able to declare that our support to Egypt in the Suez crisis would be of no avail because, as he put it, zero plus zero equals zero. Or, more recently, that the very brightest of our own children declare that the *sharī-'ah* is barbaric (the term that Romans used, to refer to non-Romans, like ourselves).

As every industrialist knows, cheap imports are disastrous for local industry. For this reason the government places restrictions on imports in order to foster industrialization. What is not realized, however, is that the same is true of ideas. At the moment we are flooded by cheap imported ideas which have driven out any local capacity for independent thought. Just as in trade, so in ideas. The more powerful countries follow a policy of regulating their own imports while pressing other countries to keep their imports open.

Falling prey to this duplicity, our intellectuals would abhor any suggestion of regulating imports of foreign news, television programmes and the like. They do not realise, however, that both political and financial censorship does take place in all countries, which proclaim themselves as bastions of liberalism. But the practices of other countries should not matter. We should decide the issue on its merits. Whether we regulate information flows generally or not, there is good reason to define the kinds of images which we should supply at public expense through publicly controlled (and financed) media. A sound information policy, consistent with a national policy on culture and an integrated strategy for defence and development must be devised and implemented.

Education Policy Equally important, though of longer gestation in terms of its effects, is the policy on education. The basic function of education, anywhere in the world, is the preservation and transmission of traditional culture; in our instance, Islamicate culture. Unfortunately, the system of education was diverted from its primary purpose during the colonial period and was instead harnessed to the distribution of patronage (by way of jobs in the bureaucracy) by the colonial powers–through regulation of intake and the establishment of a system of competitive examinations for selection into the civil service.

Today, academic institutions are seen as a place where one can acquire a degree, which opens doors to soft jobs mainly in the bureaucracy, rather than an education, much less culture. The education system has become an essential component of a dual labour market in which the largest market–civil and military bureaucracy–provides 'soft' lifetime jobs in which a large proportion of the 'wage' consists of a 'rental' or 'quasi-rental' income associated with successful entry into, and passage out of, educational institutions with very few places. Because the returns to this lottery are so high—not only in terms of income, but also in terms of security, prestige and social status—a large majority of our youth spend their twenties in an effort to crash the system, unmindful of the opportunities foregone in the private 'hard' jobs market.

In this way, we have created the classic 'rent-seeking' society in which a 'license/permit' mentality has developed, in which a pervasive personality type is being created which is motivated largely by the search of rent-seeking as opposed to wage or profit-seeking opportunities. The decision to raise the eligibility age of Central Superior Service examinations is a case in point: as a result, it becomes quite rational for a twenty-five year old to continue for five more years to try to cash in on the enormous rewards of civil service employment, rather than switching to a career in the 'hard' jobs market. The national loss associated with the existence of this lottery is incalculable.

There is a symbiotic relation between this dual system of employment and the dual structure of society. The nation cannot go on much longer on the basis of a post-colonial colonial setup in which an anglophile elite education serves as an essential mechanism of exclusion in the distribution of patronage and rent, while the vernacular class suffers the loss and indignity of leading a second-rate existence. While there is little which we can do to reform the generation which has already been educated in this system, we must begin the process of eliminating this dualism and creating a unified literate population of Muslim-Pakistanis.

A system of education, especially at the primary and secondary levels, must be instituted which provides a uniform content of education in the national language across the country. This would ensure that the next generation which emerges from this system shares the same values and lifestyles and is conversant with modern science and technology. This would also enhance political cohesion, social mobility and equality, occupational integration, and in time, promote self-reliance in technology and scientific endeavours.

This requires, however, a comprehensive redesign of the educational system so that it has the qualitative potential to produce graduates with the motivation and technical competence to fulfil expectations set for them. Education must cease to be an instrument by which the more privileged segments of society maintain their control over opportunities for power and profit, which are denied to the more capable because of their inability to master the English language.

Justice and Police   Together with a radical reform of education and information, an effort must also be made to establish effective checks on the civil and military bureaucracy by strengthening the legislature and by establishing a sound judicial and police system. The common citizen must be assured of the safety of his life, person and property, he must be confident of being able to obtain justice when wronged, and above all, have a share in the making of laws, which must widely be seen to be just. The law must be blind to the class of the citizen; the judicial process, fair; and punishment, uniform. Again, this requires the anglophile class to respect the wishes of the majority, no matter how unmodern they might seem to him.

Resisting Alien Patronage: The Road to Self-Reliance

Supplementing efforts to build consensus around an Islamicate conception of authority, a fundamental revision of economic strategy would be called for if we are to develop the capacity to resist foreign patronage. Given the long history of dependence on the West—primarily for defence, secondarily for economic assistance—and the consequent development of a large, powerful class which stands to gain by this relationship, this would have to be a gradual process. In concrete terms, it is our dependence on the United States of America, which has reached an extent which endangers both our national security and our ability to enter into a healthy relationship with other countries of the world, including the United States.

There should be no illusions about the view of Pakistan's sovereignty taken by the United States. Of the many examples, one will suffice: former U. S. National Security Adviser, Zbigniew Brzezinski (1986, p. 24) takes this view of the world: 'The most important protected allies (of the USA) are Western Europe, Canada, Japan, and South Korea. But America also has dependent clients in the Middle East (Israel and Egypt), Southwest Asia (Pakistan), and Southeast Asia (Thailand and the Philippines). The entire imperial system embraces more than 780 million people.' No self-respecting nation can continue in a status of a 'dependent client' for any length of time.

What is the source of this dependency? It is primarily our inability to defend our territory by self-reliant means. This inability arises as much from a relative lack of coercive power, as from deficiencies in our ability to extend patronage (national wealth) and, above all, in the ability of our indigenous sources of authority to command the respect of our professional elites charged with strategy formulation. An approach towards strengthening respect for indigenous authority has been outlined in some detail earlier in the monograph. We focus in this section on strengthening patronage, and in the last section on some aspects of strengthening coercive strength.

The dependence introduced by our defence predicament is carried over into our development plans. It is part of the strategic doctrine, and in some cases national laws, of our Western suppliers of arms that military assistance must be provided with economic assistance for development. They also require that economic plans be prepared, along lines fashionable among their scholars and experts, to absorb this assistance which must be spent on imports of capital goods from these countries. In this way our choices in development strategy become restricted to those compatible with the foreign policy of our major donors.

The pursuit of more self-reliant paths of economic development requires a coordinated planning of defence and development, with a much greater coordination of public and private sector efforts and less liberal trade and industrial policies in selected areas. The difficulty is that for many reasons, this would not be acceptable to our foreign sources of military equipment and development finance. In addition, as with the more radical military options, it would call for major shifts in the social and political structure, imposing great hardships on the anglophile class.

It is important to realise, however, that the present course is not sustainable for very long. Even the goals of the anglophile class are not likely to be served by the continued pursuit of a defence strategy in which we rely on indifferent allies for our security, and gain short-term defensive capability at the expense of a cumulative and growing external debt which saps our national wealth and sovereignty. The elements of a revised economic strategy to remedy the situation would be as follows:

(i)   The design of a National Policy on Culture (which is being undertaken under the Seventh Plan) which should stress the unity of the Islamicate culture of Pakistan, whose paramountcy should be left in no doubt; subservient to its Islamic character, an active development of ethnic and regional Islamicate sub-national cultures, and of the minorities, including the dominant Anglo-American sub-culture.

(ii) In support of this policy, the design of an Information Policy oriented towards the short-term fostering of cultural goals of the nation, rather than its present harmful efforts at transmitting imported images which sustain and build up alien authority and its low-credibility efforts to project the policies of the government; and of an Education Policy oriented toward the long-term goal of preserving and transmitting our Islamicate culture, in the national language, while affording an opportunity to our scholars to acquire an ability to seek scientific and technical knowledge in all languages, including English.

(iii) A major revision in industrial, credit and trade policy designed to create a military-industrial complex, with close private sector collaboration, in which the plants installed should be of a scale which provides for exports (with government support), and should be provided the benefits of protection; the military-oriented industrial policy should support the industries of tomorrow —like electronics, robotics, optics, etc.—

rather than perpetually trying to catch up with opportunities of yesterday.

(iv) Successful industrialization would require simultaneous efforts to raise agricultural productivity, which can only be done by creating the conditions in which rural labour is gradually moved to non-agricultural activities by promoting non-farm employment in rural areas, through investment in handicrafts, small industry, construction and services, and by encouraging the growth of the vernacular economy in both rural and urban areas.

(v) The reduction of alien patronage and the establishment of a more transparent system of public decision-making, in which the award of benefits to private parties by the government—through licenses, permits, tax exemptions, preferential credit, etc.--is not done by the bureaucracy behind closed doors, but is made more open, by full disclosure (after the fact, if sensitive issues of policy are involved) to public representatives at the local, provincial and federal levels.

Resisting Coercive Power

Finally, we address the question of enhancing our ability to resist coercive power, on which the bulk of the present thinking focuses—and largely does so in terms of acquisition of more imported materiel. Obviously, a radical shift in this approach cannot come about. However, given our present and expected resources in relation to those of the enemy, it is a matter of arithmetic to show that our present strategy of symmetric response is not sustainable: in any long-term projection all force ratios would continue to deteriorate beyond critically low levels, despite the accumulation of dangerously high levels of external debt owed to countries who are at best unsympathetic to our religion, culture and indeed, national survival.

There is little we can do about this situation in the short-run. Our unique geopolitical predicament places not only a heavy burden of defence on the nation, but in many ways also determines our defence strategy. Given the location of the bulk of our population and strategic points in the narrow strip between the Indus and our Eastern borders, it is not possible for us to engage in defence in depth. Nor do we have the kind of resources needed to maintain defence forces of anywhere near the size of the enemy forces. We can only hope therefore to maintain a credible deterrence, which makes us a costly morsel for the enemy to swallow.

Defence strategy therefore relies on intelligence, to provide us early warning of enemy mobilization; a pre-emptive air-strike capability and superior tactical abilities of our ground forces, to permit deep penetration in a forward defence strategy; but ultimately, on effective diplomacy, to secure a quick cessation of hostilities in the event of war. This calls for expensive imports of airborne warning systems and fighter aircrafts, together with the most modern material for ground forces, most of which are not available without special political relations with supplying countries.

As long as we are constrained to stay with this defence strategy, we cannot be self-reliant in defence to any major degree, no matter how affluent we become. There is some scope to lessen our dependence on defence imports. At present, we import the bulk of our materiel requirements. With effort this ratio can be brought down. But given the scale of optimal plants in the defence industry, a very major reduction in import requirements is not possible except in the long-term, and only where a friendly government allows the transfer of technology involved.

There are, of course, more radical ways to defend the nation. The professional armed forces can be supplemented by people's militias, more effective civil defence forces and larger reserves, in an integrated strategy for defence involving the entire population. Obviously, the nation would have to be prepared for the hardships and sacrifices that this entails. That this is not theoretical can be seen by the example of the Afghan Mujahideen who have brought a superpower to its knees in just nine years; but their commitment to Islam and their culture, and their ability to suffer hardships beyond ordinarily tolerable levels should not be underestimated. In the ultimate analysis, a nation united in its determination to resist the enemy, prepared to die for it, and exact a price psychologically which the enemy is not prepared to pay is invincible whether it has sophisticated arms or not.

More radical options, however, are not practical in our current social and political frame of mind. In practical terms, therefore, we must pursue our present strategy in the short-term, but it is imperative that we embark immediately on the asymmetric response strategy proposed in this monograph, and begin to invest in reshaping the cognitive structure of society and the pattern of economic development which will yield results only in the long-term, but which will then allow us to resist coercive power more effectively.

Given the prospect of an adverse military balance for some time to come, it is essential that innovative methods be relied upon to maximize our defence capability. First, a strategic settlement policy must be implemented to provide some depth to our defensive efforts. Second, a strategic doctrine must be formulated to ensure that the effectiveness of such coercive power as we posses is maximum; for, as Kissinger (1957, pp. 16-17) points out, history demonstrates that superiority in strategic doctrine has been the source of victory at least as often as superiority in resources.

Strategic Settlement Policy   Both defence and development considerations argue for the design of a strategic population settlement (and resettlement) policy. According to the Seventh Five-Year Plan (chapter 3):

'The urban population is estimated to reach 61 million in 2003, or almost double the present level. The additional urban population would require the development of cities two times the combined size of the present seven big cities of the country." Obviously, in the absence of a settlement policy, an unchecked growth of this dimension would cause a major breakdown of urban services, as well as a security problem in situations of conflict.

It is therefore essential that a programme is designed and implemented under which additional population on the left bank of the Indus (which presently accounts for one-third of our area but two-thirds of our population) is settled on the right bank, in order also to reduce the strategic vulnerability of the nation arising from the location of major urban conglomerates near hostile borders. This should be accomplished by opening a major transport corridor some distance away on the right bank of the Indus, leading to the port city of Ormara in Baluchistan. The government's settlement policy should be promoted by substantial investment in transportation and electricity transmission networks, as well as the development of a major port at Ormara.

A New Security Doctrine [8]   A strategic doctrine involves not only the selection of weapons systems but the elaboration of a mode of survival of society--explaining in advance the likely threats to security which might occur and preparing a response to these contingencies as a matter of routine, so that creative thought can be reserved for genuine emergencies. There is, of course, always a security doctrine--in terms of the decisions of the Joint Chiefs of Staff and the operational plans of the military services. Like the case of development strategy, however, as heads of military services these officials are participants in the bureaucratic game of budgetary appropriations and administrative management, so that what emerges is more a feasible administrative compromise than an effective national strategy.

With the establishment of the civilian order, it should now be possible for the Defence Division to give attention to a unified over-all strategic doctrine which encompasses not only the various operational plans of the services, but brings to bear the activities of intelligence agencies and the Interior Division in a comprehensive assessment of threat and formulation of response. In particular, the Defence Division needs to develop a doctrine to respond to non-conventional threats to national security, like subversion, insurgency and terrorism, in a more coordinated fashion, rather than dealing with it as a matter for domestic law and order agencies.

In addition, even in terms of a response to the more conventional threat of war, it may be worthwhile to review the extent to which our defence needs are met by the conventional division of services, patterned on conventional (Europeanate) doctrines, according to mode of transport–the Army, Navy and Air Force. Would it not be more effective to organize our defence forces in more innovative ways–for example, under three commands: an Eastern and a North-Western Command, consisting of unified army and air force units, and a Southern Command, consisting primarily of unified navy and air force units, assigned to protect the respective theatres?

Such a division would reflect the realities of the strategic situation more aptly, and could confer a strategic advantage which a straightforward comparison of force levels would not show. With the emergence of an agreed strategic doctrine in the Defence Division, security objectives would be more clearly defined at the national level, and to the narrow fiscal view of the services would be counterpoised a strategic view of the Defence Division. The Defence Coordination Committee of the Cabinet could then discuss not just the choices relating to the acquisition of the tools of war but of the most imaginative, cost-effective, ways of their use.

Too much should not be expected, of course, from organizational remedies. A great deal also depends on the style of policy-making, which is affected among other things by the agreed corpus of the 'lessons' of past conflicts (Kashmir 1948, the 1965 war, and the 1971 war), the degree of realism in the analysis of present dangers, and the extent to which we expect to rely on our 'allies' in emergency situations. For reasons of social psychology, from which the military is not exempt, we tend to be sentimental in our analyses of the past, to be less than realistic in our analyses of present dangers, and eschew boldness and innovation in the formulation of future conduct. This is compounded by habits of dependence nurtured over the last forty years, in which we tend to place unrealistic demands on our so-called allies in situations of conflict.

This raises the ultimate problem in assessing the effectiveness of security against a hostile coercive power: the adequacy of our leadership groups to confront the challenges we might confront. This also raises the more general problem faced by all societies—the need to strike an appropriate balance between the principle of organization and that of inspiration. Organization, the preservation of status quo, provides for stability; but it is inspiration, the courage to pursue a vision, which provides for growth. The national experience is confined to the level of average past experience; leadership lies in transcending average performance, and seizing the initiative in striving towards the possible well before it is proven as certain.

There is in this a fundamental conflict between the bureaucrat and the statesman. Bureaucracies, all over the world, seek safety, avoid risk, and tend to exaggerate the technical complexity of the problems, and seek to reduce the scope for exercise of judgement to the minimum. The inclination of the bureaucracy is to deny the possibility of gains from conceptual innovation, by classifying it as 'unsound', 'risky', or other characterizations which reveal a preference for stability over exceptional performance. The status quo has the advantage of being familiar; opportunities lost, can always be said not to have existed.

A weak and poor country, however, cannot eschew the gains from statesmanship. Our defence predicament demands that we maximise the effectiveness of such weapons as we have not only by a symmetric response, but by an innovative asymmetric response to threatening power. The logic of status quo and stability would not have created Pakistan; the example of the Quaid-e-Azam is not a testimony to bureaucratic methods. But it is not merely survival which is at stake. As an ideological nation, it is up to our statesmen to show the world that the tryst with Allah that the Muslims of India made early in this century will be fulfilled; that we will succeed in establishing a community in which Muslims can lead a life in accordance with the Qur'ān and the *Sunnah*, despite the constraints of a hostile cultural environment.

ANNEXURE

A Brief History of Russian Methods of Promoting Ethno-Linguistic Nationalism to Divide the Muslims of Soviet Central Asia

In the century before Muhammad ibn Qasim came to Sind, Islam had arrived in many of the areas which now constitute the Soviet Union--Azerbaijan (642) and Derbent (685), which remained in Muslim hands for many centuries; Eastern Caucasus and Trans-Caucasia, until the nineteenth century; and, to our North, the Amu-Syr Basin (673 and 706-716), including Bukhara (676 and 706-709) and Samarqand (710-712). With the irruption of the Mongols in the thirteenth century, and their subsequent coversion to Islam, Muslim rule was extended to the bulk of the area now in the Soviet Union (Benningsen and Broxup 1983, pp.2-3).

As a result, for some three hundred years before 1552, when Ivan the Terrible (d. 1584) captured Kazan the capital of the Tatar khanate on the Volga, the bulk of the areas today called Russia (including Moscow since 1382), along with Spain and the Balkans in Europe, had been ruled by Muslims (Mongols, referred to as the Golden Horde, and originally, as the Blue Horde). From

1552, the Russians expanded into Muslim lands in three phases: Expansion of the Czardom of Moscow (1552-1605); Respite (During the Western Expansion); and Conquests under the Romanovs (- 1900).

While colonialism, and the methods associated with it are not new, the Russian situation in Central Asia was unique in being the only instance in which a formerly conquered nation rose to colonise its masters. The latent 'inferiority complex' of the Russians, now masters over their Muslim populations, precluded any possibility of arriving at a sympathetic relationship with the Muslims: thus the 'nationality problem' was created in Russia and later in the Soviet Union. From 1552 to 1917, the major methods employed by the Russians to maintain control over their Muslim colonies consisted of:

- *Genocide*: either by forced expulsion--applied to the Western Cherkess tribes, the Abkhazian Muslims, and partly to the Crimean Tatars (forced to migrate to the Ottoman empire in 1865); or later, by attempted slaughter--of Turkmen tribes by General Skobelev (unsuccessful, despite the massacre of Gok-Tepe in 1881); or finally, by forced extinction through isolation--the 'dying out' *(vymiranie)* of populations, carried out with some success among the Volga Tatars (sixteenth century), the Bashkirs of Southern Urals (seventeenth century), in Northwestern Caucasus (late nineteenth century), and finally in the Kazakh steppes (late nineteenth to early twentieth century).

- *Assimilation*: through forced conversion to Orthodox Christianity–with great success, of the Volga Tatars (in the sixteenth and nineteenth centuries), and tried without success, with the Kazakhs (in the twentieth century); or through conversion to Christianity and linguistic and cultural Russification – tried with mixed results, among the Volga Tatars (for some two hundred years before 1783).
- *Non-Interference*: pursued with good results in Azerbaijan in the nineteenth century.
- *Co-option of Elite and Non-Interference with Masses*: tried with some success in Kabarda, Ossetia, and Kazakhstan.
- *Real Partnership*: offered with great success by Catherine II (the Great, d. 1796) to the Volga Tatars, and by Alexander II (d. 1881) in the Kazakh steppes.

The Revolution of 1917 was welcomed by the Muslims. The Revolution succeeded in overthrowing the yoke of the Romanovs and the Muslim communities expected it to be the first step towards national independence. In 1904-05, three Muslim congresses were held (in Nizhni-Novgorod, St. Petersburg, and again in Nizhni-Novgorod), and the first Great Pan-Muslim Congress met in Moscow on the 1st of May 1917 with 900 Muslim delegates representing all the Muslim territories of Russia. The Congress endorsed pan-Islamic pan-Turkic ideals, and held that the Muslims of Russia constituted one nation (*millet*), geographically divided into a number of states using three languages:

(i)   Tatar-Bashkir state in the Middle Volga region, consisting of 6 million people (the majority, Muslims), with Volga Tatar to be the only written language;

(ii)   A unified Turkestan, including Kazakhstan and other Central Asian territories (Uzbek, Kirghiz, Turkmen and Tajik), with Chagatay Turkic to be the only written language of this vast region; and

(iii)   Muslim Caucasus, including Azerbaijan, Daghestan and the Central-North Caucasus, with a heterogeneous population (both *Shī'a* and *Sunnī*, with Turkic, Iranian, and Ibero-Caucasian spoken languages in use), but unified by the use of Azeri Turkic as the only written language.

From 1917 to 1923, this situation was not questioned by the Bolsheviks. The term 'Muslim' was used in official Soviet texts to designate all Muslims, without ethnic or regional distinctions. One of the most important section of the Commissariat of Nationality Affairs, or *Narkomnats* (*Narodnyi komissariat po delam natsional'nostei*), created in November 1917, under the chairmanship of Stalin to mediate between disputing nationalities, was the Central Muslim Commissariat, or

Muskom. The Muslims saw co-operation with the Bolsheviks as the first step to independence. It is significant that almost fifty percent of the Sixth Red Army which held the Siberian front against Kolchak--the main front of the war–consisted of Muslim soldiers and officers (Bennigsen and Wimbush 1979, pp. 27-29).

After 1923, however, the Bolshevik leadership proceeded to break up the unified Muslim *Millet* and put the fragments together into small 'modern' Muslim nations, each one with an exact territorial demarcation, its own written official language, specially elaborated for this occasion, its own state apparatus, economic interests and even historical background and cultural traditions (Benngisen and Broxup 1983, p. 38).

As Bennigsen and Wimbush (1979, p. 82) describe it:

> Finally, in late 1922 and early 1923, steps were taken to prepare for the *razmezhevanie* ('parcel-ling') of Central Asia, the process by which the peoples of this region were divided into component nations, thereby ending once and for all the Muslim national communists' dreams of a united Muslim-Turkic state--Turkestan.

In its immediate objectives, the strategy of breaking up a unified Muslim nation into a set of ethno-linguistic nationalities has been successful. However, Muslim nationalism remains entrenched, even among Muslim communists, whose sense of Muslim cultural identity has proven to be more durable than their commitments to Muslim dogma or praxis. Nevertheless, it is instructive to

review the extent to which the Russians have gone in
their policy of fragmentation of the Muslim *ummah*
(Bennigsen and Broxup 1983, pp. 37-43):

- The *Tatar-Bashkir* state envisaged in the
  VolgaUral region was accepted by the hard-
  pressed Bolsheviks in May 1918, but with
  victory in the autumn of 1918, the Soviets
  decided to create two small republics:
  - the *Bashkir Republic* was set up on
    March 23, 1919, and provided with a
    literary Bashkir language in 1923,
    which had been a vernacular of the
    Tatar language used by the Bashkirs,
    a community of peasant mountaineers;
    and
  - a *Tatar Republic* was created on May
    27, 1920. To this day, the Bashkirs still
    consider themselves to be Tatars, and
    Russian efforts to create a Bashkir
    culture have met with little success.
- It was in what was to become *Turkestan*, the
  area directly to the North of Afghanistan,
  that Stalin prevailed over the strongest
  resistance offered by the Muslims to divide
  the region into six ethno-linguistic states:
  - The *Uzbek Soviet Socialist Republic*,
    created on October 27, 1924; with Uz-
    bek as a written language (as distinct
    from Chagatay Turkic) since 1923;
  - The *Turkmen Soviet Socialist Republic*,

created on October 27, 1924; with Turkmen being a written language close to Chagatay since the eighteenth century, and a 'modern' literary Turkmen having been created since 1924;

- The *Tajik Soviet Socialist Republic,* first created as an Autonomous Region (October 14, 1924), then an Autonomous Republic (March 15, 1925), and finally, a Federal Republic (on October 15, 1929); with Tajik, an old literary language since the ninth century;

- The *Kirghiz Soviet Socialist Republic*, created first as the 'Qara Kirghiz Autonomous Region' (October 14, 1924), then as Autonomous Republic (February 1, 1926), and finally, as a Federal Republic (on December 5, 1936); with Kirghiz as a written language, created in 1924;

- The *Kazakh Soviet Socialist Republic,* created first as the 'Kirghiz Autonomous Republic' (August 26, 1920), then as 'Kazakh Autonomous Republic' (April 1925), and finally, as a Federal Republic (since December 5, 1936); with Kazakh, a written language since the mid-nineteenth century; and

- The *Karakalpak Autonomous Republic*,created first as an Autonomous Region (February 16, 1925), and since 1936 as an Autonomous Republic; with Karakalpak, a written language created in 1925.[1]

- Finally, in the Northern, *Muslim Caucasus*, the ethnic mosaic of rugged mountaineers consisted of highly conservative Muslims unified by Islam, the widespread use of two literary languages, Arabic and Azeri Turkic, and fiercely anti-Russian sentiment. First, the Russians agreed to the foundation of a unified Autonomous Mountain Republic (*Avtonomnya Gorskaya Republica*) on January 20, 1919, but as soon as the Civil War was over, and the Chechen-Daghestan uprising came to an end (1921), the Republic was divided into five units:

- The autonomous *Republic* of the *Chechens* and the Ingush, created on December 5, 1936, by the fusion of the Chechen Autonomous Region (founded in 1922) and the Ingush Autonomous Region (in 1924); the Chechen language was promoted to a written language in 1925 and the Ingush in 1923;

- The *Kabarda Balkar Autonomous Republic*, created in December 1936, again by fusing the Kabarda Autonomous Region (1921) and the Barda Autonomous Region (1922); with both Kabardian and Balkar languages becoming written in 1924;
- The *North Ossetian Autonomous Region* was made an Autonomous Republic in 1936; initially, with two Ossetian literary languages created: 'Iron' spoken by Christian Iron tribes, and 'Digor' spoken by Muslim Digors, but in 1936, Digor lost the status of a written language;
- The *Adyghe Autonomous Region* created on July 27, 1922; with Adyghe becoming a written language in 1928;
- The *Karachay-Balkar Autonomous Region* created on January 22, 1922; with three written literary languages: the Cherkess (similar to the Kabardian), the Karachay (similar to the Balkar), and Abaza, a Cherkess dialect, promoted to the rank of literary language in 1938.[6]

NOTES

Introduction

This observation, including the phraseology, is inspired by Schelling (1958), which includes two concluding chapters on Economic warfare and strategic trade controls, and Trade controls and national security. For a more recent exploratory essay on economic warfare, along with references to other works, see Wiles (1988).

Chapter 1

1. The definition of power presented here, despite some difference of terminology and presentation, is a paraphrase of Galbraith (1983). This usage departs from the traditional use in the literature on international relations in which power is distinguished from influence. Knorr (1975, p. 3), for example, clarifies the distinction:" The relations between sovereign states assume three different forms: cooperation, conflict, and indifference... power is relevant only when inter-state relations are conflictive, not when they are cooperative (or indifferent). Influence, however, not only plays a role in situations of conflict but may also do so in the establishment, maintenance, and expansion of a purely cooperative enterprise." This definition is employed by Tahir-Kheli (1982, p. xii) in her important work on the US-Pakistan relationship. In our terminology, influence would just be non-coercive power.

2. Galbraith (1983) calls these conditioned power, compensatory power and condign (or, as suggested by Wrong (1980), coercive) power.

3. On national styles, in military policy and in the conduct of war, see Luttwak (1987, pp. 16-17, 98).

4. Throughout this paper "Europe" (or "the West"), is used for short to refer to Europe and European settlements overseas--in the Americas, Australia & New Zealand, South Africa and Israel. The adjectives, European, Western and modern (which, strictly speaking, refers to nineteenth century European conditions), are employed in the same way.

5. Although Galbraith (1983) does not use the word security, the ideas of symmetric and asymmetric response to power are his.

6. As Winston Churchill, quoted by Cohen (1987, p. 10), observed about World War I: "At the summit true politics and strategy are one. The maneuver which brings an ally into the field is as serviceable as that which wins a great battle. The maneuver which gains an important strategic point may be less valuable than that which placates or overawes a dangerous neutral."

7. This is a paraphrase of Cohen (1987, pp. 16-19).

8. Although an influential view has it that it was a feint: the intent being to draw strength to Lahore. The main effort, backed by an armoured division, came two days later in the Shakargarh salient, northwest of Lahore. I am indebted to Brig. (Retd.) Noor A. Husain for bringing this view to my attention.

9. For a guarded statement of Pakistan Army's operational strategy in the 1965 war, see Musa (1983, pp. 13-33).

Chapter 2

1. This section relies on Luttwak (1987).

2. As Clausewitz puts it: "The essential difference is that war is not an exercise of the will directed at inanimate matter, as is the case with the mechanical arts...In war, the will is directed at an animate object that reacts. It must be obvious that the intellectual codification used in the arts and sciences is inappropriate to such an activity." Quoted in Luttwak (1987, p. 16).

3. The balanced growth doctrine, as it was then called, was associated with the works of Rosenstein-Rodan (1943), Nurkse (1953), Lewis (1955), and Scitovsky (1954).

4. Albert Hirschman (1958). A reconciliation was provided by Streeten (1963). Five years after Hirschman, in Pakistan, the word strategy found itself in the title of a book by Mahbubul Haq (1963).

5. This paraphrases Hanxian (1985, pp. 33-42).

6. This is an all too short paraphrase of Moore, Jr. (1966). I have had the occasion to use this summary statement elsewhere too (see References).

7. This paraphrases Kuznets (1966), the earliest statement of the patterns school of defining development, which has been quite fashionable since then. The reader is cautioned that this precis of Kuznets' work does violence to the original, both in being selective, and in abandoning the care and caution with which he states his results.

8. It is interesting that in the question of population, an exception is made to the uniform practice under which economic development is defined to reflect faithfully the European experience. Kuznets (1966, p. 19) has this to say by way of

explanation: "The puzzle (in including population growth in the definition of economic growth) is resolved if we distinguish between the definition of economic growth as a desirable process or goal...and the definition of economic growth as it has been observed...in the past. Obviously it would be desirable for many underdeveloped countries today to minimize the increase in population and to strive for a marked rise in per capita product." Others have suggested a racial, or racist, bias to all population control proposals.

Chapter 3

1. Lt. Gen. (Retd.) Fazal Muqeem Khan, quoted in Cohen (1984, p. 123), states: "In Pakistan, at the military level, there has never been any joint planning in the true sense of the word. At best, unilaterally produced service plans have been coordinated through bilateral discussions between the services."

2. It may not be insignificant that of the working groups constituted to assist in the drafting of the Sixth and the Seventh Plans, the working group on Economic Strategy did not submit its report in both cases. Of the 55 working groups (and sub-groups) constituted for the Seventh Plan, six did not submit a report: the groups on Economic Strategy, Income Distribution Policy, Katchi Abadies, Youth Development, Sports, and Mass Media. Similarly, in the drafting of the Sixth Plan, of the 35 working groups constituted, more or less the same groups failed to submit a report: Economic Strategy & Framework, Incomes Policy, Low Income Housing, and Mass Media.

3. In late 1988, the National Economic Council (NEC) was chaired by the Prime Minister (the President has chaired the NEC when there was no Prime Minister), and consisted of

sixteen Federal Ministers, Deputy Chairman, Planning Commission, and provincial Chief Ministers, Finance Ministers, and Chairmen, Planning & Development Boards (or Additional Chief Secretaries (Development) as the case may be). It should be noted, however, that there is no constitutional bar to the President or the provincial governments nominating eminent private citizens, or members of the assemblies, to the NEC.

4. The present practice appears to be at variance with what is envisaged in the Constitution. The Constitution clearly assigns the task of formulating plans to the NEC, which it sees as an advisory, and not executive, body. In practice, however, it is the Planning Commission, constituted by executive order, which formulates the plan and submits it for NEC approval. National planning, on the other hand, is a federal subject under which the approval of projects could be placed under a body created by executive order, like the Planning Commission. However, in practice, there is an Executive Committee of the NEC (ECNEC) which considers and approves public sector development projects.

5. Except possibly for a few years under President Ayub Khan, who personally chaired the Commission, the Planning Commission has never really taken the lead in defining problems and seeking solutions. For much of the time it has simply not functioned; in other periods, it has been persuaded to attend to planning in response to initiatives by the Ministry of Planning.

6. There is a considerable literature on the link between foreign assistance and development planning in Pakistan. See, for example, Rosen (1985). About the preparation of the First Plan, for example, Rosen (1985, p. 153) reports that: "The Chairman, Zahid Husain, wrote the introductory chapter... He

wrote the controversial chapters on public administration and land reform... He also edited all drafts of all the other chapters, but much of the writing of those chapters was done by members of the Harvard Advisory Group."

7. For a description of the programme, see Aziz (1988).

8. In an article, written twenty years ago, Mahbubul Haq (1968) then Chief Economist, Planning Commission, listed "development fashions" among the seven sins of economic planners: "We have seen a number of fashions sweep the world in the last two decades. The planners are often willing victims of these changing fashions,...partly because they may end up with very little money if they do not subscribe to the current fashionable thinking in the donor countries." The situation is no different today.

9. Before the triumph of Evangelical-Utilitarianism in England, this was clear to the British as well. Sir John Malcolm, quoted in Stokes (1959, p. 24), wrote in 1823: "Great and beneficial alterations in society, to be complete, must be produced within the society itself; they cannot be the mere fabrication of its superiors, or of a few who deem themselves enlightened."

10. Once again, in a telling quote, Mahbubul Haq (1968) writes: "Many of us in the developing world emerged out of the liberal institutions of the West with a resolve to try out liberal economic policies in our countries and to deliver them from poverty and squalour. Many liberals in the West extended their helping hand,... "

Chapter 4

1. The term, Islamicate, is due to Marshall Hodgson (1974, definition, 1:57-60), on whose seminal work much of this section relies, in many instances using his phraseology, without proper attribution. The adjective 'Islamic' refers to the religion, Islam, while 'Islamicate' refers to the social and cultural complex associated with Islam and the Muslims, even when found among non-Muslims. Thus, for example, Urdu is properly not an 'Islamic' language, but an 'Islamicate' language.

2. Since our concern is to counterpoise, analytically, the evolution of high culture, society and politics in the Islamicate region with that of Europe which serves as a model for schemes of economic development and social modernization, we depart from the conventional periodization of Islamic history, and adopt (and adapt) that offered by Hodgson (1974, 1:96), which seems suitable for these purposes.

3. Hodgson (1974, 1:221n, 234) departs radically from the traditional periodization of early Muslim history, for reasons which may not be sound. His Primitive Caliphate, called here, Early Caliphate, covers the period not only of the khulafa'al-rashidun but also the Umayyads, until the death ofIbnal-Zubayr (r.) in 692 and the accession of Abd-al-Malik b. Marwan (692-705).

4. The use of Western categories in translating Islamic concepts is a source of much misunderstanding. For example din which is frequently translated as religion is much more than that; functionally, the secular equivalent of din, without its spiritual character, would be culture. Similarly, the translation of Rasul (s.) as prophet reflects the Greek idea

that messengers of Gods are characterised by their gift of prophecy, an attribute quite alien to Islamic thought; messenger, being a better translation. By contrast, *Allāh* is seldom translated as God, to cultivate the illusion that the Muslims worship a separate deity from that of Jews and Christians.

5. This has been especially true where the concept of order is based on the brief experience (from about 1789; some two hundred years only) of the European peoples (Europe, and Europeans settled overseas--in the Americas, Oceania, South Africa and Occupied Palestine; constituting perhaps one-fifth of the human race). An understanding of these difficulties has been compounded by the fact that the Europeans have seen themselves as champions of liberty, despite the very severely restricted lives they have led, by comparison.

6. This is a fundamental source of many difficultieis in creating legal systems combining the sharī 'ah with secular legislative systems. The difficulties surround not only the substance of law but also of procedure. Thus, as Hodgson (1974, 1:337) points out that for *sharī* law, precedent holds only so far as it is ethically correct; for Anglo-Saxon law, precedent holds qua precedent (for the sake of predictability).

7. Nor does this first principle make the sharī ah primitive or outdated as some critics have held. As Hodgson (1974, 1:336-37) notes: There have been some to see in the *sharī* approach to law and community life—as in much else where Islam does not make the distinctions that Europeans have made--a 'primitiveness' which they ascribe to its being developed among the Bedouins (which, of course, it was not) or at least among 'unsophisticated' Arabs. But to be at once comprehensive and simple is not primitive; indeed, it is just the

reverse. That kind of simplicity has historically been very hard to attain.

8. By *masha'ikh* we refer to persons venerated for their spiritual merit;those who are looked up to for spiritual guidence and direction.

9. This is one of the central theses of Hodgson (1974), who characterizes the social order as the *A'yān-Amīr* system, and the resulting political order as the military-patronage state.

10. Although there was agriculture, it was not the source of social and political power.

11. This is the brilliant *A'yān-Amīr* system hypothesis of Hodgson (1974, 2:64, 91-135). The term *A'yān* is more clearly recognisable as *shurafā'* in Urdu.

12. For a highly informative study of the English political mind of the nineteenth century, which is alive and well in the modern bureaucracy of Pakistan, see Stokes (1959).

13. Hodgson (1974, 1:50, 109-10) uses the term Oikoumene-- 'not just as an area term (Islamicate) but to refer to the Afro-Eurasian agrarian historical complex as having a distinctive interregional articulation in an ever-growing area. Originally, the term is Greek, where it referred to the 'i-nhabited quarter' of the world,... a geographically fixed area between Atlantic and Pacific and between the equator and the uninhabitably cold earth.'

14. This sentence is a near-quote from Ahmad (1967, p. 104), who goes on to point out that the *'ulamā'* of Deoband were successful in synthesizing the traditions of the three principal

successful in synthesizing the traditions of the three principal
centres of Muslim learning in nineteenth century India—at
Delhi (the most eminent, founded by Shah Waliallāh,
emphasizing *tafsīr* and *ḥadīth*), Lucknow (the oldest, at Farangi
Mahal, emphasizing a study of rationalism and jurisprudence
in the Transoxanian tradition, and least concerned with social
and political questions), and Khayrabad (emphasizing medieval
philosophy and logic). They were Ash'arite and Māturīdī in
dogma; Ḥanafites in *fiqh*; rejected *bid'ah* and insisted on
conformity to the *Sunnah*, but opposed not only speculative
'naturalism' of 'Aligarh but also the heterodoxy of the
ahl-i-ḥadīth. The rest of this section relies also on the seminal
works of S. M. Ikram.

15. This is, I believe, a more meaningful distinction than those
based on the European experience: like traditional-modern,
secular-religious, feudal-peasant, worker-capitalist, all of which
(I believe) are not appropriate to our context—in the empirical sense, that all variables will be more sharply divided across
the vernacular-anglophile divide than across any other
typology.

Chapter 5

1. A National Security Council was constituted by P. O. No. 14
of 1985, but was dropped by the Eighth Amendment (Act
XVIII of 1985, dated 11th November 1985).

2. These are not exhaustive. Two other notable provisions,
among others, relate to the declaration of sovereignty of Allah
over the entire universe and to Islam being the 'State religion'
of Pakistan—but the exact legal import of these provisions is
unclear. For a somewhat dated, but still highly relevant

discussion of the 'Religious, Ethical and Ideological Implications of our Constitution,' see Brohi (1958, pp. 731-99).

3. As pointed out earlier, under the Constitution, Principles of Policy are to be pursued subject to availability of resources, and no remedies are to lie against those who do not follow them.

4. For exact details see Arts. 203A, 203B, 203C, 203D. For revisional and other jurisdiction of the court, its powers and procedures, the appellate jurisdiction of the Supreme Court, and other provisions relating to the Federal Shariat Court, see Arts. 50. 203E to 203J.

5. As Ruth Benedict said of race conflict, it is not race that we need to understand, but conflict. Morris (1968, p. 167).

6. Stalin (in his article in the review *Proveshcheniye* (No. 3, March 5, 1913)) defined a nation as:"a stable community of human beings, which has accrued historically and is founded on an identity of language, territory and economy, and shares the same spiritual values." See Bennigsen and Lemercier-Quelquejay (1967, p. 249). Bennigsen and Wimbush (1979, p. 233) claim to offer a better translation: a "historically evolved, stable community arising on the foundation of a common language, territory, economic life and psychological makeup, manifested in a community of culture."

7. The implicit dogma, presented in an influential study by Banuazizi and Weiner (1987, p. 3), runs as follows: "the erosion or breakup of the traditional forms of tribal authority (leads) to the creation of new forms of ethnic identity." The idea of an 'American' social science is based on Manicas (1987).

8. This entire section relies heavily, often quoting without explicit attribution, from Kissinger (1957).

Annexure

1. In addition, three more languages were created: Uyghurs, literary language, Neo-Uyghurs, close to the old Chagatay, and Dungans, using Chinese transliterated into Cyrillic script.

2. In Daghestan the policy of linguistic fragmentation was applied even further, and some two dozen linguistic communities were created.

Bibliography

Ahmad, Aziz. 1967 . *Islamic Modernism in India and Pakistan. 1857-1964*. London. Bombay & Karachi: Oxford University Press.

Banuazizi, Ali and Myron Weiner. 1987 . *The State,Religion, and Ethnic Politics: Pakistan. Iran and Afghanistan*. Lahore. Islamabad. Karachi: Vanguard Books.

Bennigsen, Alexandre and Marie Broxup.1983. *The Islamic Threat to the Soviet State*. London & Canberra: Croom Helm. reproduced by Services Book Club. Rawalpindi.

Bennigsen, Alexandre and Chantal Lemercier-Quelquejay. 1967. *Islam in the Soviet Union*. London: Pall Mall Press. in association with the Central Asian Research Centre.

Bennigsen, Alexandre and S. Enders Wimbush. 1979 . *Muslim National Communism in the Soviet Union: A Revolutionary Strategy for the Colonial World*. Chicago and London: The University of Chicago Press.

Brohi, A. K. 1958 . *Fundamental Law of Pakistan*.Karachi: Din Muhammadi Press.

Brzezinski, Zbigniew. 1986 . *Game Plan: How to Conduct the U.S.-Soviet Contest*. Boston New York: The Atlantic Monthly Press.

Cohen, Eliot A. 1987 ." Distant Battles".In Stephanie G. Neuman and Robert E. Harkavy. *The Lessons of Recent Wars in the Third World: Comparative Dimensions*. Volume II, Lexington. Massachusets and Toronto: D. C. Heath and Company. Lexington Books.

Cohen, Stephen Philip. 1984 . *The Pakistan Army*.Berkeley: University of California Press. Also. New Delhi: Himalayan Books to which page references refer.

Deger, Saadet. 1986 . *"Military Expenditures"*. In *Third World Countries : The Economic Effects*. London. Boston and Henley: Routledge & Kegan Paul.

Galbraith, John Kenneth. 1983 . *The Anatomy of Power*. London: Corgi Books. 1985.

Hanxian, Luo. 1985 . *Economic Changes in Rural China*. Beijing: New World Press.

Haq, Mahbub ul. 1963 . *The Strategy of Economic Planning*. Karachi. Lahore.Dacca: Oxford University Press.

Haq, Mahbub ul. 1968 . "Seven Sins of Economic Planners". In Moin Baqai and Irving Brecher. 1973 . *Development Planning and Policy in Pakistan 1950-70*. Karachi: National Institute of Social & Economic Research.

Hirschman, Albert O. 1958 . *The Strategy of Economic Development*. New Haven: Yale University Press .

Hodgson, Marshall G. S. 1974 . *The Venture of Islam: Conscience and History in a World Civilization*. In 3 volumes. Chicago and London: The University of Chicago Press.

Ikram, S.M. 1961 . *Muslim Rule in India and Pakistan (711-1856 A.C.). (A Political and Cultural History).* Lahore: Star Book Depot. Educational Publication

Kissinger, Henry A. 1959 . *Nuclear Weapons and Foreign Policy.* New York: W. W. Norton & Company. Abridged Edition. 1969.

Knorr, Klaus. 1975 . *The Power of Nations.* New York: Basic Books.

Kuznets, Simon. 1966 . *Modern Economic Growth: Rate, Structure, and Spread.* New Haven and London: Yale University Press.

Lewis, W. Arthur. 1955 . *Theory of Economic Growth.* London: George Allen & Unwin Ltd.

Luttwak, Edward N. 1987 . *Strategy: The Logic of War and Peace.* Cambridge. Massachusetts and London, England: The Belknapp Press of Harvard University Press.

Manicas, Peter T. 1987 . *A History and Philosophy of the Social Sciences.* Oxford and New York: Basil Blackwell.

Moore, Jr., Barrington. 1966 . *Social Origins of Dictatorship and Democracy: Lord and Peasant in the Making of the Modern World.* Boston: Beacon Press.

Morris, H. S. 1968 . "Ethnic Groups". In David L. Sills. ed. (1968. pp. 167-72). *International Encyclopedia of the Social Sciences.* Volume 5. The Macmillan Company & The Free Press.

Musa, General (Retired) Mohammad. 1983 . *My Version: India-Pakistan War 1965.* Lahore: Wajidalis Limited.

Nurkse, Ragnar . 1953 . *Problems of Capital Formation in Underdeveloped Countries*. New York: Oxford University Press. 1967.

Rosen, George. 1985 . *Western Economists and Eastern Societies: Agents of Change in South Asia. 1950-1970*. Baltimore and London: The Johns Hopkins University Press.

Rosenstein-Rodan. 1943 . "Problems of Industrialization-of Eastern and South-Eastern Europe". *Economic Journal*. 53 (June-September 1943). Reproduced in A. N. Agarwala and S. P. Singh. ed. 1958 . *The Economics of Underdevelopment*. New York: Oxford University Press.

Schelling, Thomas C. 1958 . *International Economics*. Boston: Allyn and Bacon. Inc.

Scitovsky, Tibor. 1954 . "Two Concepts of External Economies". *Journal of Political Economy*. 62 (April 1954).

Streeten, Paul. 1963 . "Balanced versus Unbalanced Growth". *The Economic Weekly*. April 20. 1963.

Tahir-Kheli, Shirin. 1982 . The *United States and Pakistan: The Evolution of an Influence Relationship*. New York: Praeger.

Wiles, P. J. D. 1988 . "Economic War". In John Eatwell. Murray Milgate and Peter Newman. ed. (1988. pp. 77-80). *The New Palgrave: A Dictionary of Economics*. Volume 2. London: Macmillan.

Wrong, Dennis H. 1980 . *Power: Its Forms. Bases and Uses*. New York: Harper Colophon Books. Quoted in Galbraith (1983).

Zaman, Arshad. 1989 . "Dimensions of Self-Reliance".
   Journal of the Institute of Bankers in Pakistan. Vol.
   55. No.1 (March 1989).
Zedong, Mao. 1965 . "The Present Situation and Our
   Tasks". *Selected Works.* Beijing: Foreign Languages
   Volume IV. Quoted in Luo Hanxian (1985).